PROHIBITION'S
GREATEST
MYTHS

PROHIBITION'S

GREATEST
MYTHS

THE DISTILLED TRUTH ABOUT
AMERICA'S ANTI-ALCOHOL CRUSADE

EDITED BY
MICHAEL LEWIS & RICHARD F. HAMM

LOUISIANA STATE UNIVERSITY PRESS   BATON ROUGE

Published by Louisiana State University Press
Copyright © 2020 by Louisiana State University Press
All rights reserved
Manufactured in the United States of America
First printing

Designer: Barbara Neely Bourgoyne
Typeface: Sentinel
Printer and binder: Sheridan Books

Photo opposite title page: Agents pouring whiskey into a storm drain, 1921.
Courtesy Library of Congress.

Library of Congress Cataloging-in-Publication Data
Names: Lewis, Michael, 1965– editor. | Hamm, Richard F., editor.
Title: Prohibition's greatest myths : the distilled truth about America's anti-alcohol
    crusade / edited by Michael Lewis and Richard F. Hamm.
Description: Baton Rouge : Louisiana State University Press, 2020. | Includes index.
Identifiers: LCCN 2019036188 (print) | LCCN 2019036189 (ebook) | ISBN 978-0-8071-
    7038-0 (cloth) | ISBN 978-0-8071-7302-2 (pdf) | ISBN 978-0-8071-7303-9 (epub)
Subjects: LCSH: Prohibition—United States—History—20th century.
Classification: LCC HV5089 .P87 2020 (print) | LCC HV5089 (ebook) | DDC
    364.1/73097309042—dc23
LC record available at https://lccn.loc.gov/2019036188
LC ebook record available at https://lccn.loc.gov/2019036189

CONTENTS

PREFACE

This volume began at a conference in the Netherlands when a few prohibition scholars were collectively bemoaning the gap between what historians know about prohibition and what much of the public believes about it. Noting that the one hundredth anniversary of federal prohibition was only a couple of years away, these scholars decided to use the occasion to put together a short volume addressing some of the most consistently misunderstood aspects of the prohibition era. Our initial goal was to make sure that readers had the story right; nothing bothers an expert more than others not fully understanding what it is they know.

As the contributors to the volume were finishing their essays, potent signs about how disruptive alcohol is in our society gave this topic renewed urgency. In a public hearing before a vast audience connected to the scene electronically, a US senator and a nominee for the US Supreme Court questioned each other about whether they drank to the point of memory loss or blackout. Just a week earlier, the World Health Organization had released a massive report on the ill effects of alcohol. It declared that more than 3 million people died because of harmful use of alcohol in 2016. Further, the WHO concluded, "alcohol caused more than 5% of the global disease burden." Yet, in response to the manifest problems caused by alcohol today, there is no movement seeking to ban alcohol in the United States or throughout much of the world.

One reason for the lack of such a movement today is that prohibition, especially the American experience of national prohibition, is widely perceived to have been a colossal failure. Without a doubt, the nationwide effort to ban alcohol in the United States failed, but much of what occurred during the prohibition era has been obscured and hidden by myths. The authors of this volume seek to lift the veils of myths both to allow a fuller understanding of the past and to guide the public and policymakers regarding other controversial and potentially dangerous commodities. It is hoped that separating myth from reality about prohibition will enable our society to better cope with these commodities as well as with alcohol.

Like shot glasses on a bar, these essays can be imbibed in whatever order (and at whatever speed) readers find most enjoyable.

MYTH 1

TEMPERANCE ADVOCATES AND PROHIBITIONISTS SHARED THE SAME GOALS AND TACTICS

H. PAUL THOMPSON JR.

It seems as if every time I tell people that I research the temperance movement they make some comment about Al Capone, Carrie Nation, or the Woman's Christian Temperance Union. I usually respond by saying, "No, I study the *nineteenth-century* temperance movement." My response elicits blank stares. Apparently, the nineteenth-century antebellum-reform, or "Benevolent Empire" section, of everyone's US history textbook leaves little to no impression on students. Popular memory about the temperance movement seems to begin somewhere around 1900 and moves quickly to the drama of national prohibition in the 1920s. Popular books and media attract our attention with titillating stories of rum running, organized crime, corrupt law-enforcement officers, and alcohol-related violence. Popular documentaries like Ken Burns's *Prohibition* and books like the recent *Last Call: The Rise and Fall of Prohibition* often omit the less colorful parts of the century-long movement or fail to capture its nuances and complexities, perpetuating an overly simplified, one-dimensional image of the movement. This image often leaves one bewildered, at best, about how Americans could

ever have banned such a historically ubiquitous and culturally norma-
tive article of trade and consumption as alcoholic beverages.

Popular culture has made it easy to buy into the myth that temperance reformers and prohibitionists were one and the same. While it is
true that the rhetoric of early twentieth-century prohibitionists often
conflated the two, it is also true that many temperance reformers rejected the goals and tactics of prohibitionists. Temperance was a large,
multifaceted movement, and as such, *temperance reformer* was an um-
brella term for a wide range of reformers working to limit or ban the
consumption of alcoholic beverages. One subset of this group was prohibitionists, who, directed and coordinated by the Anti-Saloon League of
America (ASL), guided from start to finish the passage of the Eighteenth
Amendment and the Volstead Act, thereby creating national prohibition. Temperance began as an idea in the 1780s, and over the years it
encompassed a variety of goals, rationales, and strategies, not to mention
successive generations of leaders, rank-and-file reformers, and organizational structures. The movement evolved throughout the nineteenth
century as activists continually debated their rationales, goals, and tactics. Temperance reformers were as divided among themselves—sometimes vehemently—as other reformers often were. Temperance played a
critical role in advancing women's rights and was implicated in a range
of class, ethnic, religious, scientific, and political discourses. It was also a
prominent theme in literature, entertainment, and popular culture.

The temperance movement was quintessentially American if for no
other reasons than that it remained a "work in progress" for so many
years, and because its adherents maintained a running debate about their
goals and how best to achieve them. Prior to the beginning of national
prohibition in January 1920, the rise of the ASL in the 1890s represented
the single most profound watershed moment in the movement's history. The ASL initiated and led the national campaign for the Eighteenth
Amendment, and the dominance and success of its rhetoric and tactics
represented such a significant break from longstanding temperance
practices that it is more accurate to think of the 1890s as the end of the
temperance movement and the beginning of the prohibition movement.[1]

This essay looks at the origins of temperance ideas and then discusses the movement's nineteenth-century evolution from an organizational perspective to contrast its complexity with the narrow, laser-like focus of the ASL and the campaign for the Eighteenth Amendment.

ANTEBELLUM TEMPERANCE REFORM

Americans' annual per capita alcohol consumption increased markedly during the late eighteenth and early nineteenth centuries. By 1830, annual per capita consumption of absolute alcohol had reached almost four gallons, more than twice what it was in the late twentieth century. One of the first persons to perceive this trend was Benjamin Rush, a respected Revolutionary Era medical doctor. In 1784 he published *An Inquiry into the Effects of Spiritous Liquors on the Human Body and Mind,* where he argued that distilled beverages like rum and whiskey were unhealthy and dangerous and that instead people should drink healthy beverages like beer, wine, and ciders (all of which were hard then). Rush's work prepared the ground for the next generation of temperance advocates. By the second decade of the nineteenth century, thousands of local temperance societies had sprung up across the nation, many with the active support of local clergy. Sponsoring speakers, distributing literature, and pledge signing were their primary activities. They believed that through "moral suasion"—appeals to one's reason—they would eventually persuade more and more Americans to abstain from both drunkenness and distilled beverages.[2]

Although several preachers published sermons attacking drunkenness and distilled drinks during these early years, none rivaled in influence those preached and published in the mid-1820s by Lyman Beecher, an important revivalist of the Second Great Awakening. Through these and other sermons, Beecher articulated the theological foundations for temperance and other reforms of the antebellum period. For revivalists like Beecher, benevolent reforms drew on the same theology they employed in their revivalist preaching. They emphasized the individual's free will but also one's accountability to God about how one used that will. Revivalists wanted nothing to distort one's free will, or reasoning faculties, and thus compromise their ability to respond to the preacher's call to repentance and conversion. Equally important was the widely held view at the time that America needed virtuous citizens if it was to become a successful, long-lasting republic. Beecher argued that there were three ways for one to develop those virtues: through a religious conversion experience, through obedience to righteous laws, or through the influence of positive social pressures. Reform societies, like temperance societies, were a means of creating positive social pressures leading to virtuous and patriotic citizens.[3]

Beecher's *Six Sermons on the Nature, Occasions, Signs, Evils, and Remedy of Intemperance* (1827) became as influential in the temperance movement as his daughter's *Uncle Tom's Cabin* would become in the abolitionist movement. These sermons issued the first public call for three things that would characterize the movement for decades to come: (1) defining temperance as abstinence from all intoxicating beverages (not just distilled, or "ardent," spirits); (2) a national organization to coordinate the movement; and (3) an intentional effort to educate public sentiment so that voters would eventually call for the outlawing of the traffic in intoxicating beverages. Beecher's sermons sought to defeat the "enemy" of intemperance, namely, individuals' self-destructive behavior, not a "system."[4]

The first attempt at nationally coordinating the movement began in Boston in February 1826, with the founding of the American Temperance Society. As an overtly evangelical Protestant organization, the society merely sought to persuade already temperate individuals to abstain from distilled spirits. Rather than restoring drunkards, it simply sought to help sober people remain sober. Demonstrating its effective mass appeal, by 1835 the society had organized more than 1.5 million people (about 12 percent of the nation's free population) into more than eight thousand local societies. There were likely still more unaffiliated local societies. Many societies were age group, employment, race, or gender specific. Temperance reformers during these years were generally involved in multiple reforms; for example, fourteen of the original sixteen members of the American Temperance Society were also members of the American Tract Society and the American Board of Commissioners for Foreign Missions. Temperance was easily the most popular reform in this period, transcending most socioeconomic and regional distinctions.

Jonathan Leavitt, in an 1830 address before the New York Young Men's Society for the Promotion of Temperance, captured the spirit of the temperance movement at this point when he said that already temperate persons should seek to persuade others because "its whole force is that of reason. The influence of laws and magistrates it does not embrace." Reuben Walworth, president of the New-York State Society for the Promotion of Temperance, speaking of the "demon of intemperance," argued that no law could do what an "enlightened public sentiment" could do. He maintained that prohibition laws could not deliver people from their own responsibility "until an intelligent and virtuous community shall arise and vindicate their own privileges. We have a right to protection from this species of depredation, but this right no lawgiver can exercise for us. Our deliverance must be of our own deed." Reformers knew it would take time to develop this kind of public sentiment, and they were in it for the long haul.[5]

In 1836 the American Temperance Society renamed itself the American Temperance Union, and after a heated debate it approved and recommended to local societies a new pledge, the teetotal pledge. This new pledge redefined temperance as abstinence from *all* intoxicating beverages. Although made in response to several local societies that had already switched to the teetotal pledge, this decision created much backlash for the organization. Many accused the movement of becoming fanatical. Opposition to the pledge, coupled with the recession of 1837, dried up much funding and halted the growth of the movement, although the American Temperance Union limped along until 1865.[6]

After the American Temperance Society and the American Temperance Union, local evangelical churches and parachurch organizations were probably the most influential temperance voices in antebellum America. The American Tract Society and the American Sunday School

Union published and distributed much temperance literature. Missionaries sent out by the American Board of Commissioners for Foreign Missions (to American Indians), the American Baptist Home Mission Society, and the American Missionary Association all preached temperance and organized local societies throughout the western part of the nation. Older Congregational and Presbyterian churches and newer evangelical groups like the Methodists and Baptists, alongside Quakers, preached against drunkenness and disciplined their members for drunkenness, if not for drinking. Many African Methodist Episcopal churches created temperance societies for their members. Popular revivalists such as Charles Finney and Peter Cartwright railed against drunkenness and urged converts to become active in the movement. Finney was so proud of his promotion of temperance during his Rochester revival that he bragged that he had made it an "appendage" of the revival because he expected all converts to sign the pledge.[7]

In these early years of the movement, its explicitly Christian character was on display for all to see. The masthead of the *Journal of Humanity and Herald of the American Temperance Society* printed out the text of Proverbs 14:34: "Righteousness exalteth a nation; but sin is a reproach to any people." Justin Edwards, one of the founders of the American Temperance Society, advised temperance workers, "Let your object be the glory of God in the Salvation of men." The executive committee of the American Temperance Union asserted that God himself was the "supporter and director" of the movement and that temperance was a "mighty moral and religious movement, going forth from hearts imbued with the spirit of the Gospel." Reformers would have agreed with Thomas Grimke, president of the Charleston, South Carolina, Temperance Union, that temperance was a "peculiarly Christian" reform.[8]

Yet another set of temperance organizations emerged after 1840. The first was the Washingtonians, a working-class movement that used secular methods to reach the masses. Clergy, the middle class, and the wealthy generally criticized and avoided the movement, but in 1841 they claimed to have persuaded hundreds of thousands of working men to sign the teetotal pledge and to have reformed many drunkards. They sponsored picnics, fairs, and parades, pioneered the use of reformed-drunkard testimonials, and generally re-created the male camaraderie of tavern life. A variety of internal conflicts led to the fracturing and rapid decline of the movement, but its members had successfully popularized the movement in the urban working-class world. As the Washingtonians struggled, new temperance lodges began to appear. Such groups as the Sons of Temperance (1843), the Independent Order of Good Samaritans (1847), and the Independent Order of Good Templars (1852) often operated as secret societies, required members to sign abstinence pledges, incorporated formal rituals and regalia, provided personal accountability, and sometimes offered the insurance benefits of a mutual-aid society. Groups like the Masons and the Odd Fellows, while not requiring an abstinence pledge, expected nonabstinent members to drink temperately and avoid public drunkenness.[9]

Simultaneous with this redefinition of the temperance movement was the rise of the legal prohibition movement. The 1833 convention of the American Temperance Society passed a resolution condemning the "liquor traffic" as morally wrong and recommended that "local communities be permitted by law to prohibit the said traffic within their respective jurisdictions." Passed over strong opposition, this resolution subtly and gradually shifted the object of the reformers' wrath from personal habits of intemperance to the liquor traffic itself, or the entire retail liquor business. Some who opposed this measure argued that only personal religious transformation, not a law, could make someone abstinent, while others argued that pushing for a prohibition law implied the failure of moral suasion. Supporters, however, argued back that prohibitory laws would eventually make the selling of liquor as despised by respectable people as were brothels and gambling establishments. They further maintained that reformed drunkards needed a society in which access to alcohol was not easy. Finally, prohibitionists argued that some people were just so obstinate that only the weight of the law would make them realize the evil of their ways, whether they were selling or consuming. The focus on local political action meant that prohibition would only be attempted in locales where there was already sufficient public sentiment to support it, support presumably created through moral-suasion efforts. This approach reflected America's strongly democratic culture. Following some local successes, reformers turned their activism toward statewide prohibition, but moral-suasion rhetoric and practices remained a parallel theme among reformers. For example, after calling for the end of the liquor traffic, Dr. J. Henry Clark, secretary of a New Jersey temperance society, reminded readers that "we are by no means to forget the original quiet mode of reaching the conscience by moral suasion."[10]

The first example of statewide restrictive legislation was Massachusetts's infamous 1838 Fifteen Gallon Law, which required all distilled liquor to be sold in quantities of fifteen or more gallons. The electoral backlash was strong. Voters replaced the governor and so many legislators that the new government immediately repealed the law. Similarly, restrictive efforts elsewhere faced political opposition, and in some cases prohibitionists and their property were subject to violence. Then in 1851, under the leadership of Neal Dow, the mayor of Portland, Maine, and founder of the Maine Temperance Union, Maine passed the first statewide prohibition law. The success of this law inspired activists in many states, and by 1855 twelve states had passed their own version of the "Maine Law," but again, because of so much opposition, by the end of the decade most state laws had been repealed or judicially gutted. Instances of mob violence connected with the enforcement of these laws also tarnished the movement's image. Where the laws remained on the books, enforcement was generally lax. One of the most important aspects of the context of these laws was the increasing Irish and German immigration, which was especially noticeable in urban areas. Much of the opposition to prohibition came from these communities, to whose cultural traditions whiskey and beer drinking were central. Such laws often pitted native-born Protestants against immigrant Roman Catholics, thus aiding and abetting the rise of the xenophobic Know Nothing Party.[11]

CONTINUITIES IN POSTBELLUM TEMPERANCE REFORM

In August 1865, in the wake of the Civil War, hundreds of temperance reformers regrouped at the Fifth National Temperance Convention to debate the future of their movement, only to expose all of their old divisions. Some criticized churches for not doing enough to support the movement, and some called for prohibition laws and the election of officials who would enforce them. Others called for a more active educational campaign based on the publication and distribution of literature and argued that prohibition would never work without the existence of a strong public sentiment. Many speakers seconded the sentiments of the convention chairperson, who employed rhetoric from the early republic when he reminded the delegates that "virtue alone exalted the nation." In the end, the delegates passed several resolutions, including one calling for an education campaign designed to inspire people to call for prohibition, and they created the National Temperance Society & Publication House (NTS&PH) out of the former American Temperance Union. The NTS&PH published and distributed massive amounts of inexpensive and free literature and defended every community's right to conduct local option elections, but it refused to endorse any specific prohibition campaign. Beginning in 1881 the NTS&PH turned most of its attention toward freed slaves in the South.[12]

Despite the organization's apolitical stance, several of its leaders wanted more, and in 1869 they joined disaffected temperance reformers from the Republican Party to found the Prohibition Party. Most temperance people had supported the Republican Party since its founding and were proud of their party's role in the destruction of slavery. After the war, some expected the Republican Party to prioritize prohibition, but once they realized that was not going to happen, they wanted another party to lead what they believed was the nation's next great moral crusade. The new party's platform called for several progressive reforms, including direct election of senators and woman's suffrage. Women party members could participate on equal terms with men by nominating candidates, drafting the platform, and voting for convention delegates. The Prohibition Party peaked in strength relative to the other parties in the 1884 presidential election but never presented a serious challenge to the nation's two-party system. Despite internal debates about narrowing its focus, the Prohibition Party remained committed to multiple reforms. Few reformers forsook their own political party, so the Prohibition Party remained a fringe group with little influence.[13]

The last national temperance organization to organize prior to the 1890s was the Woman's Christian Temperance Union (WCTU), which grew out of the 1873–74 Women's Crusade, in which thousands of women in hundreds of town prayed and sang outside saloons, causing hundreds to close, at least for a few months, and many men to sign the abstinence pledge. Veterans of the movement organized the WCTU in Cleveland, Ohio, in November 1874. Although committed to petitioning and lobbying for prohibition laws, the organization reached the zenith of its influence in the 1880s under the leadership of Frances Willard, who touted the "Do Everything" motto, encouraging local chapters to respond to whatever needs they saw in their individual communities. WCTU chapters not only canvassed in support of local option elections but also worked to reduce crime, address public-health concerns, visit the sick and incarcerated, and educate children about the dangers of alcohol. Willard began to speak out for the enfranchisement of women so that they could protect the purity of their homes by voting to close saloons. Local chapters elected representatives to state conventions, and state conventions sent delegates to national conventions. This approach, combined with the charismatic leadership of Willard, created a decentralized, democratized, and highly energized national organization with chapters in more than half of the nation's counties.

One of Willard's most consequential decisions was to place Mary H. Hunt over its Department of Scientific Temperance Instruction, which worked tirelessly to persuade virtually every state to pass mandatory "scientific" temperance instruction guidelines for all public schools and to persuade all publishers of physiology textbooks to devote 25 percent of each book to alcohol and drug education. However, the accuracy of the information often left much to be desired. Willard increasingly aligned the WCTU with the Prohibition Party, but this created so much friction that finally in 1889 J. Ellen Foster led a breakaway faction to form the Nonpartisan WCTU, with the goal of focusing solely on prohibition laws.[14]

In the post–Civil War era, evangelical Protestant churches doubled down on their support for teetotalism. With the exception of most Lutherans, Episcopalians, and Roman Catholics, by the 1880s virtually all Christian denominations had standing temperance committees that regularly lamented the negative effects of drinking and intemperance, urged strict discipline of drinking church members, and called for various kinds of prohibitory legislation. In 1869 the devout Methodist dentist Thomas Welch had applied Louis Pasteur's recently invented pasteurization process to fresh grape juice and created the first preserved nonalcoholic grape juice, hoping that churches would use it instead of wine for Holy Communion. As soon as the WCTU organized, it launched a successful campaign to persuade churches to use Welch's grape juice. A common church sentiment at the time was expressed by the Baptist Convention of the state of Georgia, which said that preachers and laymen should take the lead in forming a "public sentiment that shall make the manufacture and sale of ardent spirits odious, so much an offense against the well-being of society."[15]

As church support for teetotalism grew after the Civil War, moral-suasion efforts remained near the top of the list of priorities for reformers, and two of the three national temperance organizations included prohibition as only one of a cluster of reforms they advocated for while working within traditional, democratically structured institutions. Even with these diverse approaches, few would have criticized the mission of the Pennsylvania State Temperance Union to "by purely moral and scriptural methods enlighten the people, and secure the practice of total abstinence by individuals and prohibition of the traffic by the state."[16]

The rise of these organizations inspired a second major nationwide push for prohibition. This time reformers targeted state constitutions. In the 1880s eighteen states held referenda on constitutional prohibition, and one state voted on statutory prohibition. Voters defeated prohibition in twelve states, and in the states where it passed, it was overturned within a few years. Alternatively, some states passed general local option laws that created standard guidelines for local communities to vote themselves dry. The largest cities in each state typically remained wet, to the consternation of rural communities, which frequently complained about the "wet" votes of urban immigrant groups and African Americans. In 1887, in the wake of prohibition defeats in Texas, Tennessee, and Atlanta, the Reverend Theodore Cuyler, president of the NTS&PH, reminded reformers of their long-held position that moral and legal suasion must go hand in hand: "No suppressive laws can be enacted or enforced unless there is a stiff public sentiment behind them. . . . If we do nothing to remove the drinking usages, they will, by their unchecked volume, not only prevent the passage of prohibitory statues, but would sweep down all legal barriers like bulrushes in a cataract." Reformers remained convinced of the necessity of persuading individuals not only to be personally abstinent but also to vote for prohibition. However, this approach did not work, and by the nineties the aging leadership of the three main national organizations increasingly struggled with internal divisions and/or declining revenue. The movement seemed as fractured as ever, but the times were changing and about to yield a new organizational approach.[17]

THE RISE OF THE PROHIBITION MOVEMENT

The many failed state referenda of the 1880s were followed in the 1890s by the overturning of prohibition in some states, such that by 1903 only Maine, Kansas, and North Dakota were still legally dry. At the same time, an increasing number of rural counties and smaller municipalities had become dry. Ironically, per capita consumption of beer was rapidly increasing at the same time. In the early nineties the movement was clearly stagnating before the 1893 founding of the Ohio Anti-Saloon League and the organization in 1895 of the Anti-Saloon League of America. These two organizations pioneered a completely new approach to the temperance movement that was reflective of their times.

The 1880s and 1890s were characterized by a small number of corporations' rapidly expanding in size, assets, and power relative to others. Corporations experimented with increasingly aggressive and sophisticated organizational structures. Historians have dubbed it the age of the "organizational revolution," as every conceivable group, from individual professionals, to competing businesses within one industry, to reformers of all stripes, formed an association to leverage the power of its numbers to promote their common interests. This was the era of the rise of government bureaucracies, which were designed to create organizational continuity and stability and maximize the benefits of professional and managerial expertise. It was increasingly common for public rhetoric to place value on the "public interest," as compared with private interests, and one outgrowth of this sentiment was the rise of "trust-busting." Business trusts were monopolies created to control prices and trade and to maximize profits in a particular industry at the expense of smaller businesses and consumers' best interests. One manifestation of this tendency to form associations was the United States Brewers' Association. Although founded during the Civil War to resist federal taxation of brewers, through the 1870s and 1880s it actively opposed prohibition as it spread across America, community by community. In a parallel effort, whiskey distillers organized their own industry organizations. One would think it would have been in the interest of brewers and distillers to jointly oppose prohibition legislation, but the two groups seldom saw eye to eye regarding the nature of the threat and failed to consistently present a united front.[18]

Howard Russell, an attorney turned preacher, who canvassed for Ohio's 1888 Local Option Bill while a theology student at Oberlin College, began to conceive of ways to address the disarray in the temperance movement using the tactics of the liquor industry itself, and of modern industry broadly speaking. After a few years of ministry in the Midwest, exposure to alcohol-related social problems, and much soul searching, Russell decided to commit himself to the cause of prohibition. He returned to Ohio in 1893 and organized the Ohio Anti-Saloon League. Russell made several critical decisions that altered the course of the movement. He followed the lead of J. Ellen Foster and the struggling Nonpartisan WCTU and made the Ohio ASL strictly nonpartisan. The ladies of the Nonpartisan WCTU supported the new Ohio ASL in various ways, including financially. Russell astutely noticed the influence businessmen could have with elected officials of both parties, and he determined to pursue the same kind of influence for prohibitionists.[19]

Second, by 1893 Russell and other temperance workers, especially one of its first employees, the lawyer Wayne Wheeler, crafted a persuasive public narrative about the "liquor trust" that exaggerated its unity and influence. Liquor-industry efforts to resist prohibition had become bigger than life to prohibitionists, so he decided to make the league primarily about closing down the liquor business per se. It was one simple goal that all reformers could agree on, with no distracting issues.

Third, modeling Russell's efforts after cutting-edge business practices, the ASL's early leaders created a bureaucratic, not democratic, organization that altered temperance conventions. Previously, temperance conventions had prioritized speeches, resolutions, and voting. They had been exercises in grass-roots democracy. The ASL, however, held conventions that were more like carefully staged pep rallies. The ASL leadership selected the leaders of local leagues; they were not elected by members. The ASL developed a permanent staff, and members of local leagues were expected to support the organization by donations, volunteering on election days, and distributing literature. ASL members did not vote and send their influence upward in the organization; rather, high-level leaders directed members' activities. The ASL organized about one hundred local leagues in Ohio in Russell's first year.

Politically, the league's strategy was to look for the "low hanging fruit" to make a name for Russell's organization and identify ASL friends in the legislative and executive branches. For example, early on Russell found a legislator to support a local option bill that he thought would be defeated. It *was* defeated, but the league made the most of the defeat by blaming it on the powerful "liquor trust" and identifying each lawmaker who had opposed the bill. Then he found a legislator who had opposed the bill and worked to defeat his renomination, and then he bragged about it. ASL literature soon made it clear that the organization cared only about whether lawmakers supported its legislation. A legislator's party affiliation, religion, and drinking habits were irrelevant. This was a radical new approach for prohibitionists, who had previously assumed that only personally abstinent elected officials would vote for and enforce prohibition laws.

News about the work spread rapidly, and reformers from around the country expressed interest in forming a new national political organization. Delegates to a convention in Washington, DC, in 1895 organized the nonpartisan Anti-Saloon League of America to coordinate the suppression of saloons throughout the nation by appropriating the strategy of the Ohio ASL. Seeking to include all temperance organizations in its leadership, the ASL of America invited all temperance groups and even denominations to appoint a person to its board of directors. The NTS&PH and the Prohibition Party refused the offer and remained at odds with the ASL.

In 1894 Russell told a reporter that strong public sentiment against drink was important and that "without public demand no law can be passed, and it is worthless when it is passed." To this end, the Ohio ASL published and distributed a huge volume of literature explaining all the reasons why the liquor business in America needed to be ended. In 1896 its monthly paper, the *American Issue,* began publishing weekly. Despite these publishing efforts, it was clear that the ASL "built its broad and successful coalition by targeting the 'saloon evil' rather than attacking personal alcohol consumption" as nineteenth-century reformers had done. Keeping to the movement's religious roots, ASL leaders regularly visited pastors, seeking to make every church a local ASL chapter under its pastor's leadership. Because of the strength of Russell's church support, ASL called itself the "Church in Action against the Saloon."

The ASL began writing model pieces of legislation and finding legislators who would sponsor them. It became expert at promoting loyalty to itself and its own agenda over all other interests and groups. It executed what we would now call get-out-the-vote drives on election days and flooded the mails with propaganda to support its anti-saloon agenda, mailing literally tons of literature every year, while constantly appealing for financial donations. The ASL found that frequently they could defeat an opponent in a close election just by an effective get-out-the-vote campaign. The number of carefully selected elections won, not the number of personal abstinence pledges signed, became the measure of success. A major turning point for the Ohio ASL occurred in 1906, when it successfully defeated a popular incumbent prohibitionist governor who had vetoed an ASL-sponsored bill because he disagreed with the league about its wording. Overnight, elected officials began to fear the league, and within two years its support was considered essential for those seeking statewide office in Ohio.

The ASL of America eventually replicated that feared status at the level of the US Congress. The ASL of America reorganized itself a few times as it worked to shore up support among reformers and win multiple drives for state prohibition. Through ASL and others' efforts, a wave of states embraced statewide prohibition. By 1913, when those states were added to local option territory, about half of Americans lived under some version of prohibition, so in that year the ASL leadership announced that it was time to launch a campaign to create national, constitutional prohibition. ASL leaders had always claimed that national prohibition was their goal. Because of its experience at the state level, it knew how to identify friends in Congress, ensure their reelection, and oppose the candidacies of their foes. From 1913 forward, they artfully employed their accumulated political expertise, their massive publishing and propaganda capacity, their successful fundraising tactics, their feared reputation, and the national spirit of self-sacrifice and anti-German sentiment inspired by World War I to elect a pro-prohibition Congress and pass the Eighteenth Amendment. The most important leader in the whole campaign was Wayne Wheeler, who became general counsel for the ASL of America in 1915. Wheeler had a well-deserved reputation for pioneering political hardball tactics, which he employed to achieve ASL legislative priorities in Congress.

The second decade of the twentieth century—the height of the Progressive Era—was an extraordinary period in American history. The US Senate and House passed the Eighteenth Amendment in the fall of 1917, and although the states had seven years to ratify it, it took them only thirteen months. The Eighteenth Amendment was the third of four constitutional amendments approved during this decade. The only period that compares to it is the era of Reconstruction, in the 1860s and 1870s. Historians have spilled much ink trying to define the Progressive Era, for it embraced many disparate themes. The passage of national prohibition reflected at least two key themes of the period. First, it aligned with the tendency of some reformers to look to increased federal-government involvement to address problems. Second, it drew on the optimism and environmentalism that were central to the ethos of the Progressive Era. Progressive reformers were generally optimistic about their ability to reform the behavior of citizens, and they worked assiduously to attack what they viewed as indirect causes of social problems. These problems included such things as poor housing, poor sanitation, lack of urban recreation opportunities, and, of course, the presence of saloons. The values of progressivism provided the ideal soil for national prohibition legislation to flourish; but it was a brief moment in time. The campaign for the Eighteenth Amendment began in 1913 and ended in 1919.

The ASL, the embodiment of the prohibition movement, was clearly *not* identical to the nineteenth-century temperance movement; rather, it is best understood as the beginning of modern American politics as we know it today. Howard Russell had created the nation's first single-issue pressure group and pioneered the method of interaction between citizens and democratically elected officials that Americans take for granted today. Commitment to nothing but specific pieces of legislation, while ignoring all other allegiances, was a brand new approach to American politics. Prohibitionists replaced the enemy of personal intemperance with the enemy of the saloon, or the liquor traffic. Given the times, it turned out to be a politically savvy move, but neither in style nor in substance did it fully distill the more expansive vision of a century of temperance-reform activism. Those earlier generations had either rejected prohibition outright, equated the work of persuading individuals to abstain with the work of ending the liquor trade, or viewed successful moral suasion as a necessary precursor to legal prohibition. Prohibitionists were a critical part of the temperance movement, but they were only *part* of it.

NOTES

1. Jack S. Blocker Jr., *American Temperance Movements: Cycles of Reform* (Boston: Twayne, 1989).

2. Lebbeus Armstrong, *The Temperance Reformation, its History from the Organization of the First Temperance Society* (New York: Fowlers & Wells, 1853), 18–27, 134–44.

3. Allan M. Winkler, "Lyman Beecher and the Temperance Crusade," *Quarterly Journal of Studies on Alcohol* 33 (1972): 939–57; Lyman Beecher, *A Reformation of Morals Practicable and Indispensable: A Sermon Delivered at New-Haven on the evening of October 27, 1812* (Andover, MA: Flagg & Gould, 1814); Beecher, *The Practicability of Suppressing Vice, by Means of Societies Instituted for that Purpose: A Sermon Delivered before the Moral Society in East Hampton (Long Island) September 21, 1803* (New London, CT: Samuel Green, 1804).

4. Lyman Beecher, *Six Sermons on the Nature, Occasions, Signs, Evils, and Remedy of Intemperance* (Boston: T. R. Marvin, 1829).

5. H. Paul Thompson Jr., *A Most Stirring and Significant Episode: Religion and the Rise and Fall of Prohibition in Black Atlanta, 1865–1887* (DeKalb: Northern Illinois University Press, 2013), 19, 28; Jonathan Leavitt, *An Address on Temperance to the Young Men of the United States, on the Subject of Temperance* (New York: Clayton & Van Norden, 1830), 16; *Fourth Annual Report of the New-York State Society for the Promotion of Temperance* (Albany: Packard & Van Benthuysen, 1833), 88; Jonathan Kittredge, Esq., *The Christian's Duty to the Temperance Cause* (Philadelphia: Baptist General Tract Society, [ca. 1820]), 8.

6. Blocker, *American Temperance Movements*, 21–25.

7. Thompson, *A Most Stirring and Significant Episode*, 29–41; Othniel A. Pendleton, "Temperance and the Evangelical Churches," *Journal of the Presbyterian Historical Society* 25 (March 1947): 14–45.

8. William A. Hallock, *Light and Love: A Sketch of the Life and Labors of the Rev. Justin Edwards, D.D.* (New York: American Tract Society, 1855), 321; *Seventh Annual Report of the American Temperance Union, in Permanent Temperance Documents of the American Temperance Society,* vol. 2 (New York: American Temperance Union, 1852), 21; Thomas S. Grimke, *Address on the Patriot Character of the Temperance Reformation* (Charleston, SC: Observer Office Press, 1833), 5.

9. Blocker, *American Temperance Movements*, 39–51.

10. J. Henry Clark, *The Present Position and Claims of the Temperance Enterprise* (New York: Baker & Scribner, 1847), 14–17.

11. Blocker, *American Temperance Movements,* 51–60; Thomas R. Pegram, *Battling Demon Rum: The Struggle for a Dry America, 1800–1933* (Chicago: Ivan R. Dee, 1999), 24–42.

12. *Proceedings of the Fifth National Temperance Convention* (New York: J. N. Stearns, 1865); Thompson, *A Most Stirring and Significant Episode,* 99–107.

13. K. Austin Kerr, *Organized for Prohibition: A New History of the Anti-Saloon League* (New Haven, CT: Yale University Press, 1985), 41–44; Lisa M. F. Andersen, *The Politics of Prohibition: American Governance and the Prohibition Party, 1869–1933* (New York: Cambridge University Press, 2013).

14. Ruth Bordin, *Woman and Temperance: The Quest for Power and Liberty, 1873–1900* (Philadelphia: Temple University Press, 1981).

15. Michael A. Homan and Mark A. Gstohl, "Jesus the Teetotaler: How Dr. Welch Put the Lord on the Wagon," *Bible Review,* April 2002, 28–29, retrieved from https://members.bib-arch.org/bible-review/18/2/6; Minutes of the 51st Anniversary of the Baptist Convention of the State of Georgia (1874), 16–17, Special Collections, Jack Tarver Library, Mercer University, Macon, GA.

16. James Black to Joshua L. Baily, 11 January, 1877, Box 2, Joshua L. Baily Collection, Special Collections, Haverford College, Haverford, PA.

17. Theodore Cuyler, "Some Plain Words on Prohibition," *Advance* 22 (10 November 1887): 705.

18. John D. Buenker, John C. Burnham, and Robert M. Crunden, *Progressivism* (Cambridge, MA: Schenkman, 1977), 3–30.

19. My portrayal of the Anti-Saloon League draws from the following works: Blocker, *American Temperance Movements;* Pegram, *Battling Demon Rum;* Kerr, *Organized for Prohibition;* Lisa McGirr, *The War on Alcohol: Prohibition and the Rise of the American State* (New York: Norton, 2016); James H. Timberlake, *Prohibition and the Progressive Movement, 1900–1920* (New York: Atheneum, 1970); and Peter Odegard, *Pressure Politics: The Story of the Anti-Saloon League* (New York: Columbia University Press, 1928).

MYTH 2

RELIGIOUS CONSERVATIVES SPEARHEADED THE PROHIBITION MOVEMENT

JOE L. COKER

When he wrote about the history of the prohibition era, Richard Hofstadter insisted that it would be an injustice to associate the Eighteenth Amendment with the progressive movement, which was going on at the same time. Instead, prohibitionism was what he called a "pseudoreform, a pinched, parochial substitute for reform" that was only supported by "a certain type of crusading mind." He went on to explain that the movement had not been spearheaded by the progressive thinkers who had brought about reforms such as child-labor laws, the minimum wage, and so on, but had instead "been carried about America by the rural-evangelical virus."[1] The association of the prohibition movement with backwoods, unenlightened, fire-and-brimstone-preaching, evangelical yahoos by this preeminent historian has since become a boilerplate explanation of the roots of America's failed experiment with regulating alcohol consumption.

Subsequent historians have frequently painted the movement as one that was primarily reactionary in nature. As the historian Dewey Grantham would later put it, the prohibition movement (along with the anti-evolution movement) was driven primarily by southern evangelical fundamentalists who were "alarmed by the growing secularization of their society" and sought to turn back turn back the hands of time by legislating liquor and evolution out of existence.[2] Thus a myth has long existed that we primarily have religious conservatives to thank for imposing prohibition upon America. There has, of course, always been much to support this characterization of prohibition. Theologically conservative evangelical Protestants have been fervent advocates of the movement to curtail America's drinking ever since the early nineteenth century and strongly supported the passage of the Eighteenth Amendment.

My own initial exposure to this interesting chapter in American history began when I was a seminary student. I was working in the cataloging department of Emory University's theology library, where I was tasked with helping catalog a massive collection of temperance hymnals. I hadn't even known such a thing existed, but it turns out that there was a whole subgenre of hymnals that provided songs to rally support for temperance and prohibition. With titles like *The Martha Washington Temperance Songster* and *Trumpet Notes for the Temperance Battle-Field,* these works reaffirmed in my mind the stereotype of prohibition as a movement that was part and parcel of the exuberant evangelical awakenings of the nineteenth century and the backward-looking fundamentalism of the early twentieth. An amusing and intriguing anecdote from one of my church-history professors, though, helped me see that there was much more to this movement than meets the eye. When I mentioned these temperance hymnals to her, she told me that her grandmother had been an ardent teetotaler and member of the Woman's Christian Temperance Union since way back. One day my professor goaded her grandmother a little bit by remarking, "You know, Grandma, the Bible tells us that Jesus himself drank wine and even turned water into wine." Without missing a beat, her grandmother responded: "I know he did, and I think the less of him for it!"

This surprising and amusing response belies something deeper that was going on in the temperance and prohibition movements in the nineteenth century and into the twentieth. Years later I would come across a nineteenth-century Baptist preacher who seemed to concur with my professor's grandmother. He remarked that if Jesus and his disciples had known then what folks in the nineteenth century knew about the dangers of alcohol consumption, they would have consumed coffee or tea at the Last Supper instead of wine.[3] Supporters of prohibition saw themselves as helping to usher in a new, enlightened, progressive era in which not only individuals but society as a whole would make forward strides in morality, health, societal well-being, and economic prosperity.

Prohibitionists were not simply conservatives who were discontented with the changing mores of society and hoped to impose some archaic, puritanical code upon the nation. (Indeed, Puritans themselves were less rigid in their attitude toward alcohol consumption than were later prohibitionists. The original Puritan settlers of Massachusetts Bay brought with them a hearty supply of ale and liquor aboard their ship *The Arabella,* and the Puritan leader Increase Mather once famously declared that alcohol was "a good creature from God.")[4] Instead, the prohibition movement always received support—and votes—from many who saw the movement as a modern, progressive, enlightened policy. It was not a coincidence that in 1919 not only did the United States embrace prohibition but so did Canada, Finland, and Norway. This was not solely the work of religious fundamentalists but rather evidence of a widely held consensus among social reformers and progressives in North America and Europe that curbing alcohol consumption was key to making social, economic, and political improvements in an industrialized, urbanized, post–World War I world.

The myth that prohibition's success was driven by religious conservatives is only partially true and misrepresents the broad appeal that liquor reform had in America in the nineteenth century and through the 1920s. It also fails to capture how prohibition legislation was understood in this era by its supporters and how the use of legislation to control what people consume still functions today. The temperance and prohibition movements were remarkable in part for their ability to draw together a diverse set of supporters, including individuals who would be labeled both conservatives and liberals, fundamentalists and progressives, pre-

and post-millennialists, evangelical and mainline Protestants, Protestants and Roman Catholics, Christians and non-Christians. A cursory look at four stages in the path that led to the Eighteenth Amendment will reveal that a strong progressive element had been present in the temperance impulse as early as the eighteenth century and throughout its development. We'll look first at how the foundations of the movement were laid in the late eighteenth century, then at the temperance movement in the first half of the nineteenth century, then at the growing prohibition movement in the second half of that century, and finally at the early twentieth-century push for nationwide prohibition.

EIGHTEENTH-CENTURY ORIGINS

Prior to the American Revolution, most Americans—Christian or otherwise—agreed with Increase Mathers's assessment of alcohol as a "good gift from God." Drinking distilled liquor was commonplace among the upper, lower, and middle classes in both the North and the South. Conventional wisdom in this era held that liquor had many beneficial properties, contributing to good health and providing energy to laborers. The first person to question such cultural assumptions was the Philadelphia physician Benjamin Rush. Most famous as a signatory of the Declaration of Independence and as surgeon general to the Continental army, Rush was very much shaped by the Age of Reason, in which he lived. A man of science, Rush decided to scientifically investigate the claims made about alcohol's positive attributes and to explore its potential negative impact. In 1784 he published *An Inquiry into the Effects of Spirituous Liquors upon the Human Body, and Their Influence upon the Happiness of Society.* This work dismantled widely held ideas in the medical community about the positive attributes of alcohol and found, instead, that drinking distilled liquor led over time to both physical disease and moral vices, including idleness, fighting, anarchy, and murder.[5]

The immediate context of Rush's exposé of the dangers of hard liquor was his concern for the fledging new nation. He feared that while

fermented drinks like wine and beer promoted cheerfulness and camaraderie, widespread consumption of "ardent spirits" could endanger
the republic because of the vice and immorality it produced.[6] But Rush
was not calling for the denizens of the new democracy to return to some
sort of biblical morality. Instead, he believed that rejecting strong beverages was the natural progression of human scientific discovery and enlightenment. He predicted that by the early twentieth century all people
would shun distilled liquor just as they already refuse to drink poison.[7]

Rush's admonition to Americans to lay off the hard stuff received a
tepid response in his own lifetime. He was a full generation ahead of
widespread public acceptance of his finding that liquor was damaging
to body, mind, and society. While few seem to have read Rush's *Inquiry*
in the eighteenth century, in the nineteenth it would be reprinted numerous times by advocates of the burgeoning temperance movement in
America, and Rush would posthumously earn the title "Father of Temperance."[8] Rush continued to advocate for moderation in one's drinking
throughout his life, but not as a religious conservative seeking to rain
on others' immoral parade. His attack on distilled liquor was driven
not by an interpretation of the Bible but rather by his Enlightenment-
influenced faith in science and his concern for the young republic he
helped found.

Rush was well ahead of his time when it came to discovering the
physical threats posed by excessive alcohol consumption, but this was
just one way in which he was trailblazing and progressive for his era. He
was also one of the earliest advocates of using exercise (such as walking,
running, and even dancing) as a means of improving one's health and
supported the education of women.[9] More importantly, Dr. Rush was an
early and outspoken critic of slavery in the United States. Well before
it was considered acceptable to do so, he published a pamphlet attacking slavery and the slave trade, effectively becoming one of the earliest
abolitionists in America.[10] Rush also espoused ideas that are deemed
progressive even now, such as opposing capital punishment regardless of
the severity of the crime.[11] The man who laid the foundation for all subsequent attacks on liquor usage in this country, then, was by no means a

religious or social conservative but rather a liberal and progressive voice in his context. When the temperance and prohibition movements took off in America in the nineteenth century, they too would be led as much by progressives as by conservatives.

THE EARLY NINETEENTH CENTURY

While Rush had laid the foundation, a widespread anti-liquor movement did not arise in America until after the War of 1812. Early temperance advocates agreed with Benjamin Rush that beer and wine were acceptable in moderation and urged abstinence only from distilled liquor. And like Rush, they did not call for legal prohibition of these beverages but rather conducted a campaign of moral suasion intended to enlighten and change the attitudes of men toward drinking. When an extensive canal system began to be built in the Northeast, it allowed for easy transportation of distilled grain to the cities along the seaboard. The ensuing "whiskey glut" led to what has been described as a "national binge," with per capita consumption of distilled spirits increasing from 2.3 gallons in 1790 to almost twice that in 1830.[12] (Present-day per capita consumption in the United States is about .75 gallons.)[13] Hard liquor was cheap and plentiful in the growing cities, and it became increasingly common for men to imbibe excessively. Thus the number of arrests for public drunkenness, brawling, and other related crimes began to spike. People began to take note of this and to form temperance societies in an effort to curtail such activities.

Many of those who led and joined such societies were evangelical Christians, of course. This was, after all, the heyday of the Second Great Awakening, and this spike in drunkenness was antithetical to the aims and values of those who were promoting the revival of religion in America. But many of the early leaders of such societies were the middle- and upper-class employers of the working men who were participating in the national binge and consequently becoming less reliable workers. For example, when Charles Finney brought religious revival to Rochester, New

York, in the early 1830s, a disproportionate number of entrepreneurs and shop proprietors attended his revival services and experienced religious conversion. Subsequently, they signed on to the temperance campaign and began to look forward to a time when, as one Baptist editor put it, "men will have done employing intemperate mechanics, and when ardent spirits will cease to distract, disturb, and ruin."[14] Temperance reform had both practical and financial benefits for the wealthier class. Those driven by economic motives, by religious motives, and by medical and social-improvement motives participated coequally in the burgeoning temperance movement. It would ultimately become a major reform movement of the century, but it would be inaccurate to characterize it as a movement led primarily by those with a conservative religious agenda.

During this period the temperance movement relied heavily upon Benjamin Rush's *Inquiry* to provide scientific backing for its campaign. The movement also retained the progressiveness of Rush by being deeply connected to the burgeoning abolitionist movement in the North. In fact, the movement often had critics in the conservative, slaveholding South because it was viewed as a twin of abolitionism and a back-door tactic by northern "liberals" to undermine slavery. The connection between these two movements became increasingly clear: William Lloyd Garrison's groundbreaking anti-slavery newspaper, the *Investigator,* merged in 1829 with the nation's longest-running temperance newspaper, the *National Philanthropist.* Just a year prior, the cousin of the slave-revolt leader John Brown had published a work explaining the parallels between intemperance and the slave trade, and by the 1830s Connecticut Baptists were proclaiming that "every man has a right to be sober and a right to be free."[15]

Those (mostly northern) evangelical Christians who embraced both temperance and abolition tended to be of the more optimistic, progressive, forward-looking ilk rather than the stereotypical backward-looking, hell-fire-and-brimstone killjoys. Temperance and abolition were tied together because these evangelicals saw them as the two major sins in American society and therefore the two major barriers to ushering in God's kingdom on earth. Slaveholding and rampant drunkenness were seen as incompatible with heaven on earth, so they both must go. Later on, conservative evangelicals in the twentieth century (and still in the twenty-first) would abandon this optimism about improving society and ushering in heaven on earth. They mostly became (and remain) premillennialists, believing that the kingdom of God on earth will be ushered in by Christ's return, not by human reform efforts prior to Christ's return. So the motives and desires of religious conservatives in the nineteenth century were quite different than those of later (and modern) Christian fundamentalists, who want to legislate people's moral behavior.

THE SECOND HALF OF THE NINETEENTH CENTURY

In the middle of the nineteenth century the anti-drinking movement made a pivotal shift that would forever alter the movement: the embrace of legal prohibition. Up to that point the temperance movement had relied upon making the moral, religious, social, and economic case for the dangers of alcohol. (Fermented drinks like beer, wine, and cider—which Rush and other early activists found acceptable—had by midcentury been added to the list of verboten drinks.) In 1851, however, the state of Maine passed a law prohibiting the manufacture and sale of most alcoholic beverages within the state.[16] Though temperance advocates had successfully achieved localized prohibition legislation in towns and counties around the country, this was the first statewide prohibition legislation in America. It would become a model embraced by eleven other states in the 1850s and by more states at the beginning of the twentieth century, setting the stage for the next logical step: nationwide prohibition. The man responsible for the passage of the "Maine Law"—as it and all such bills in other states were known—was Neal Dow. Dow, a wealthy, self-made businessman who became mayor of Portland, wrote the bill and almost single-handedly shepherded its successfully through the state legislature. Dow then traveled the country touting Maine's achievement and encouraging other states to adopt similar legislation.[17]

Raised in a Quaker family, Dow was not driven to support prohibition by evangelical religious views, nor did he rely much on religious or biblical arguments to make his case for prohibition. Instead, Dow framed the issue of prohibition in terms of economics and personal betterment and used blistering personal attacks on opponents of prohibition as a tool in making his case.[18] This early phase of legal prohibition in Maine and around the country was driven more by concerns about the effects of drinking upon the effectiveness and productivity of the working class, especially the immigrant population. Dow and other promoters of prohibition downplayed the moral and religious arguments and focused instead on the social and economic costs associated with drinking.[19] While many religious conservatives (primarily in the North, since southerners were still suspicious of connections between prohibitionists and antislavery) applauded and supported the expansion of Maine Laws, they were not the driving force that created the first statewide prohibition law in America. The prohibition laws that were passed in the 1850s were short-lived, most of them being struck down in the courts as violating the states' constitutions, and the Civil War distracted the nation from prohibition legislation throughout the 1860s and into the 1870s. When the prohibition movement began to pick up steam again in the final decades of the nineteenth century, a powerful new force within the movement emerged: women.

The Woman's Christian Temperance Union, founded in 1874 in Ohio, became a powerful social and political force in the decades that followed. It served as the primary vehicle through which women in America participated in the debate over prohibition legislation in the years leading up to the Eighteenth Amendment. Within a few years of its founding, the WCTU had more than 27,000 members, and by the end of the century it claimed more than 150,000 members, making it the largest women's organization in the world at the time.[20] This development marked a new chapter not only in the movement but also in American culture; prohibition provided American women with their first foray outside the home sphere and into the public political arena. While the WCTU's membership was, as the name implied, Christian women, many of them would not have been labeled as conservative by the standards of their day. The movement was breaking new ground for women. Their early activities involved collecting massive stacks of signed petitions to Congress and state legislatures in favor of prohibition legislation, as well as having a very public presence at the polls on election day whenever local or state-wide prohibition measures were on the ballot, trying to influence the votes of the men in their community.[21] Before long, though, the WCTU would be advocating for women to actually vote themselves, and it would become a launching pad for many leaders of the women's suffrage movement of the early twentieth century.

In 1879 Frances Willard became president of the WCTU and began to push the organization's goals and tactics in increasingly progressive directions. She later embraced Christian Socialism and advocated a "Do Everything" agenda that included not only prohibition but also prison, education, and labor reform.[22] She also embraced the controversial issue of women's suffrage. Having been introduced to socialism while visiting England, Willard set the rapidly growing prohibition organization on an increasingly progressive and liberal trajectory.[23] Though Willard was from the evangelical Methodist tradition, this leading female prohibitionist of the nineteenth century did not fit the mold of being socially conservative or theologically rigid. She rankled the conservative, male leadership of her own denomination, the Methodist Episcopal Church, regularly. When the WCTU asked Willard to address the 1880 general conference of that denomination, there was a significant uproar. The idea that a woman would address the male leaders of the denomination seemed scandalous to some in the group. Ultimately, a vote was held and a majority agreed to let Willard speak, though she opted to decline the invitation in order to avoid further confrontation.[24] The male-only group's consternation over the idea of Frances Willard speaking authoritatively about prohibition to them reflected the unease that more conservative elements in America felt regarding the growing women's suffrage movement. And it was abundantly clear to all that this new phase of the prohibition movement—and the growing presence of women at its helm—was anything but conservative or traditional. Instead, it was (as the anti-alcohol movement had always been) a forward-looking and progressive movement that was often ahead of its time.

THE EARLY TWENTIETH CENTURY

By the beginning of the twentieth century, numerous states were embracing statewide prohibition, especially in the South and the Midwest, where evangelicals were strongest. At this point in American history a rift was emerging within Protestantism that was rapidly dividing it into two harshly opposed camps: a more liberal (or "modernist," as they tended to be called) group who believed that the church had a responsibility not only to address spiritual matters but also to work for social and economic improvement, and a more conservative (or "fundamentalist," as they began to call themselves) group who believed that the function of the church was only to save souls, not to improve people's earthly existence. This division within American Protestantism is still rather pronounced today, more than a hundred years later. The theologically conservative Christians (many of whom to this day regard even casual drinking of alcohol to be a sin) are the ones who have long been associated with the passage of the Eighteenth Amendment. Indeed, they were certainly big supporters of the push for national prohibition. They generally tended to be more legalistic and backward-looking—these were the same people who brought about the Scopes trial because they did not want evolution taught to schoolchildren. Conservative evangelists of the early twentieth century like Billy Sunday traveled the country and hit the radio waves preaching against the sinfulness of alcohol and admonishing Christians to vote for prohibition.

It was hellfire-and-brimstone-preaching conservatives like Sunday who fueled the later characterization of prohibitionism as part of the "rural-evangelical virus" mentioned above. But support for an antiliquor constitutional amendment was much broader than that. In fact, prohibition was one of the only issues in the early twentieth century that bridged the growing chasm between the religious right and the religious left. Leading the prohibition cause were some of the most liberal and progressive Protestant preachers and theologians of the era. The Social Gospel was an element of the liberal, modernist impulse in American Protestantism. According to the Social Gospel, Christians had a duty to not just save souls but also improve the social and economic conditions in which people lived and therefore strongly advocated for reforms like child-labor laws, workplace-safety regulations, the establishment of a minimum wage and a forty-hour work week, and even socialism. Leading Social Gospellers also strongly supported nationwide prohibition. Leaders of the Social Gospel movement such as Josiah Strong and Charles Stelzle advocated a more liberal theology that called for progressive economic reforms in America and also viewed prohibition as a vital reform.

One of the most vocal advocates of the Social Gospel was the Baptist theologian Walter Rauschenbusch. He believed that American capitalism was deeply unchristian in its ethics and its treatment of the working class, and he called for bringing America's economic system into harmony with the ethics of Jesus. Rauschenbusch, who had served as a pastor in Hell's Kitchen in New York City for eleven years before becoming a professor, embraced socialism and sought to mobilize the church to engage in social reform.[25] In addition to completely overhauling America's capitalist system, Rauschenbusch also strongly urged the country to embrace prohibition. This liberal theologian championed the cause of prohibition because he saw the alcohol industry in America as typical of the kind of greedy capitalism that willfully destroyed lives in the pursuit of profits. Rauschenbusch emphasized the negative impact of liquor upon workers, not only the moral and economic impact but also the physical. He argued that the modern, mechanized factories of the early twentieth century were no place for inebriated workers, who were putting themselves and their coworkers at risk by imbibing during the day or working with a hangover.[26] Others from the theological "left," including the urban social reformer Jane Addams, staunchly supported prohibition as a key to improving the lives of the poor.

The eventual passage of a constitutional amendment banning the sale and manufacture of alcohol did not occur simply because of the efforts of individual pastors or theologians, whether conservative or progressive. Rather, an organization called the Anti-Saloon League (ASL) was the main force that brought about the passage of the amendment and its eventual ratification by the states. Founded in Ohio by Howard Russell, a lawyer turned Congregationalist minister, the ASL worked hard to foster its image as a pragmatic, goal-oriented organization focused solely on the passage of prohibition legislation at all levels.[27] It did not seek to replace or compete with either of the major political parties, nor did it take a side in the growing division within Protestantism between modernists and fundamentalists. Instead it drew support from both sides and managed to successfully bring together a strong coalition of supporters of prohibition. One of the key leaders of the ASL, and one of the single most important figures in the successful passage of the Eighteenth Amendment, was Wayne Wheeler. Wheeler's opposition to liquor stemmed not from religious conservatism but from the more progressive evangelical tradition ingrained in him at his alma mater, Oberlin College (which was also where Russell had done his theology degree).[28] The ASL announced in 1913 that it had set its sights on getting a prohibition amendment passed, and it took advantage of events in the following years to recast the public perception of prohibition and mobilize a broad base of voters, who in turn elected a Congress in 1916 that contained a record number of drys.[29] By December 1917 the ASL had made good on its four-year-old promise: Congress passed the Eighteenth Amendment. Numerous social, economic, and political factors contributed to the passage of the amendment (and its subsequent ratification by 46 of the 48 states), and it would be a gross oversimplification to say that it was purely the work of religious conservatives.

CONCLUSION

Looking back, then, at the push to limit people's access to liquor in America, one sees that the movement's most important leaders and shapers were not conservative evangelical Christians in the way that we often mischaracterize prohibition supporters. Instead, they were individuals motivated by edgy and progressive ideas—some of them quite liberal and controversial in their day—about how to improve society and minimize social ills. They were not driven by a desire to impose biblical values, curtail people's leisure-time activities, or impede changing moral values. By our standards today, of course, we might quickly lump many of these reformers in with fire-and-brimstone revivalists of the Second Great Awakening and the doctrinaire and dogmatic fundamentalists of the early twentieth century because they all seem "conservative" by twenty-first-century standards. But to do so would be to misrepresent the actors involved in the prohibition movement and to misunderstand their motives. It would also obfuscate just how broad-minded and progressive many of the leaders of the movement were. And this impulse to blame religious conservatives for the failed attempt at prohibiting alcohol in this country completely mischaracterizes the appeal prohibition had to a wide range of Americans a hundred years ago.

In fact, one might draw comparisons to today's culture of wanting to use government force (through high taxation or outright ban) to stop Americans from consuming any number of products. Just as was the case a century ago, todays prohibitors do not all fall conveniently into one camp. Politically liberal or progressive politicians have supported bans or restrictions on numerous products in recent years, from smoking tobacco to e-cigs to trans-fatty foods and super-sized soft drinks. Social conservatives and religious conservatives, meanwhile, tend to reject many of these bans but support things like banning abortion, upholding existing restrictions on local liquor sales, and resisting any legalization of marijuana usage. Jessica Warner's study of the promotion of abstinence—whether from alcohol, drugs, premarital sex, gambling, dancing, tobacco, or various other substances and activities—finds that it is an impulse that has been embraced by people from across the theological and ideological spectrum. The religious right, she points out, "does not have a monopoly on abstinence."[30]

Surveying American society and politics today, one finds no shortage of voices from a variety of ideological perspectives who want to regulate what you put into your body and the kinds of leisure-time activities you participate in. Some base their argument on moral grounds (which is often the case with religious conservatives who want to ban something), while some make arguments in the name of public health or costs to society (which is often the case with liberals or progressives). People of various backgrounds remain confident that the consumption of products such as tobacco, marijuana, trans-fats, and so on, can successfully be reduced or eliminated through government ban or taxation. Both liberals and conservatives are driven by a belief that such prohibitions will save lives and improve American society. Likewise, one hundred years ago a great variety of Americans—Christian conservatives and Christian liberals, political conservatives and political liberals—found common cause in the movement to prohibit alcohol. To perpetuate the myth that the passage of the Eighteenth Amendment was the work primarily of religious conservatives is to miss out on the complex and fascinating story of prohibition in America. It also hinders us from recognizing how similar impulses to regulate what people put into their bodies still shape the religious and political culture of America today.

NOTES

1. Richard Hofstadter, *The Age of Reform: From Bryan to F.D.R.* (New York: Vintage Books, 1955), 289–90.

2. Dewey Grantham, *The Life and Death of the Solid South: A Political History* (Lexington: University Press of Kentucky, 1988), 79.

3. See John Broadus, *Life and Letters of John Albert Broadus,* ed. Archibald Thomas Robertson (Philadelphia: American Baptist Publication Society, 1910), 427; and Rufus Spain, *At Ease in Zion: Social History of Southern Baptists, 1865–1900* (Tuscaloosa: University of Alabama Press, 2003), 180.

4. Quoted in W. J. Rorabaugh, *The Alcohol Republic: An American Tradition* (New York: Oxford University Press, 1979), 30.

5. Benjamin Rush, *An Inquiry into the Effects of Spirituous Liquors on the Human Body, to Which is Added, A Moral and Physical Thermometer* (Boston: Thomas & Andrews, 1790), 12.

6. Thomas R. Pegram, *Battling Demon Rum: The Struggle for a Dry America, 1800–1933* (Chicago: Ivan R. Dee, 1999), 14–15.

7. Eric Burns, *Spirits of America: A Social History of Alcohol* (Philadelphia: Temple University Press, 2004), 56.

8. Alyn Brodsky, *Benjamin Rush: Patriot and Physician* (New York: St. Martin's, 2004), 268–69.

9. Brodsky, *Benjamin Rush,* 97.

10. Brodsky, *Benjamin Rush,* 86–87, 116.

11. Brodsky, *Benjamin Rush,* 291–92.

12. W. J. Rorabaugh, "Estimated U. S. Alcoholic Beverage Consumption, 1790–1860," *Journal of Studies on Alcohol* 37 (March 1976): 362.

13. National Institute on Alcohol Abuse and Alcoholism, *Surveillance Report #95: Apparent Per Capita Alcohol Consumption; National, State, and Regional Trends, 1977–2010,* accessed 21 June 2018, https://pubs.niaaa.nih.gov/publications/Surveillance95/CONS10.htm.

14. Paul E. Johnson, *A Shopkeeper's Millennium: Society and Revivals in Rochester, New York, 1815–1837* (New York: Hill & Wang, 2004), 106–7, 121.

15. Heman Humphrey, *Parallel between Intemperance and the Slave Trade: An Address Delivered at Amherst College, July 4, 1828* (Amherst: J. S. and C. Adams, 1828); C. C. Pearson and J. Edwin Hendricks, *Liquor and Anti-Liquor in Virginia, 1619–1919* (Durham, NC: Duke University Press, 1967), 88n57.

16. Cider was excepted from the law because being primarily a rural drink, it was not connected to concerns about urban drunkenness and crime.

17. James A. Morone, *Hellfire Nation: The Politics of Sin in American History* (New Haven, CT: Yale University Press, 2003), 285.

18. Franke L. Byrne, *Prophet of Prohibition: Neal Dow and His Crusade* (Madison, WI: State Historical Society of Wisconsin, 1961), 11.

19. Ian R. Tyrrell, *Sobering Up: From Temperance to Prohibition in Antebellum America, 1800–1860* (Westport, CT: Greenwood, 1979), 273.

20. Barbara Leslie Epstein, *The Politics of Domesticity: Women, Evangelism, and Temperance in Nineteenth-Century America* (Middletown, CT: Wesleyan University Press, 1981), 90–96.

21. Ruth Bordin, *Woman and Temperance: The Quest for Power and Liberty, 1873–1900* (New Brunswick, NJ: Rutgers University Press, 1990), 51–55.

22. Ruth Bordin, *Frances Willard: A Biography* (Chapel Hill: University of North Carolina Press, 1986), 159.

23. Carolyn DeSwarte Gifford, "For God and Home and Native Land: The WCTU's Image of Woman in the Late Nineteenth Century," in *Women in New Worlds: Historical Perspectives on the Wesleyan Tradition,* ed. Hilah F. Thomas and Rosemary Skinner Keller (Nashville: Abingdon, 1981), 315–17.

24. Bordin, *Frances Willard,* 160–61.

25. Sydney E. Ahlstrom, *A Religious History of the American People* (New Haven, CT: Yale University Press, 1972), 801–2.

26. James H. Timberlake, *Prohibition and the Progressive Movement, 1900–1920* (Cambridge, MA: Harvard University Press, 1963), 24–25.

27. K. Austin Kerr, *Organized for Prohibition: A New History of the Anti-Saloon League* (New Haven, CT: Yale University Press, 1985), 77.

28. Justin Steuart, *Wayne Wheeler, Dry Boss: An Uncensored Biography of Wayne B. Wheeler* (Westport, CT: Greenwood, 1970), 38.

29. Pegram, *Battling Demon Rum,* 135–46.

30. Jessica Warner, *All or Nothing: A Short History of Abstinence in America* (Toronto: McClelland & Stewart, 2008), 1–3.

MYTH 3

THE PROHIBITION AMENDMENT AND SUPPORTING LAWS SOUGHT TO BAN INDIVIDUAL DRINKING

LISA M. F. ANDERSEN

It was 1917, and Senator Thomas Hardwick, a Georgia Democrat, issued a challenge to his colleagues. No friend of prohibition himself, his patience tried after listening to senator after senator pontificate on how the so-called prohibition amendment would end drunken debauchery, Hardwick finally rose to point out a problem: the amendment's text did not make alcohol consumption illegal. Was this simply an oversight? If the amendment were to include a ban not only on the "manufacture, sale, importation, exportation, and transportation" but also on the *consumption* of alcohol, he noted, then "*that* is complete prohibition, practical prohibition." Anything less than such a clear statement of the amendment's aims would be "utterly and totally insincere and uncandid," and Hardwick therefore proposed that consumption immediately be added to the list.[1]

Hardwick's ostensibly helpful suggestion was what contemporaries called a "joker amendment," one designed not to increase candor about the amendment's purpose but instead to sink the prohibition amendment before it was launched. His colleagues were not amused by this showboating. Yet the confusion Hardwick *pretended* to feel is now rampant among modern Americans. Libertarians, for example, assume that the Eighteenth Amendment must have been about banning consumption when they use persistent Prohibition Era drunkenness as evidence that it is futile to legislate against human desires. Liberal reformers likewise assume that the Eighteenth Amendment was primarily an anti-consumption vehicle when they contend that prohibition's overscrutiny of drinking habits—a precedent to modern drug wars—explains the slow development of social policies addressing the structural problems wrought by poverty.

Some parts of our distorted national memory of the Eighteenth Amendment are easily corrected; we need only glance at the amendment's language to know that consumption was never banned. But left unresolved would be a still more intriguing set of questions, those provoked by consideration of the breech between our national folklore and the actual legislation: What was it that the Eighteenth Amendment's advocates really wanted, if not an end to alcohol consumption? Or, if they wanted an end to alcohol consumption and its ancillary vices, why did they not ask for it?

To better understand the quick and coordinated way in which the Senate disposed of Hardwick's proposal, and why they did so, one first has to understand the pressure group under whose influence the Senate had acted. The Anti-Saloon League of America (ASL), which had initiated the campaign for a national prohibition amendment, could be quite persuasive.

THE ANTI-SALOON LEAGUE AND THE
SALOON MENACE, 1893–1913

Between the predictable positions—zealots' position that drinking was a terrible sin and inebriates' defense of personal liberty—sat a large group of politicians who cooperated with the Anti-Saloon League for pragmatic reasons. Some feared that they would otherwise lose their seats, while others appreciated how this pressure group helpfully mobilized their bases. These politicians knew that the ASL had secured a series of campaign triumphs since its founding in 1893, mostly because the league's leaders had aggressively publicized every dry success for which they could feasibly take credit, whatever the actual level of their involvement.[2] Organized as the "Church in Action against the Saloon," the ASL coordinated the messaging of Christian ministers while at the same time bringing these ministers into conversation with hardworking attorneys, prominent philanthropists such as John D. Rockefeller Sr., and some advocates for labor, such as Charles Stelzle. Within its first decade, the ASL organized in forty states and territories, and its national periodical, *American Issue,* claimed five hundred thousand mostly middle-class readers.[3] The ASL, in other words, was a big deal.

What attracted the attention of these ministers, attorneys, philanthropists, labor organizers, and hundreds of thousands of small donors was a narrow focus on the saloon as the source of national decline.[4] This shared conviction that saloons were a menace was grounded in more than a little reality. Though lionized by some as the "poor man's club," when Americans described a semipublic drinking place as a "saloon," they generally meant an establishment with little of a German beer garden's familial charm or a hotel bar's refinement.[5] The "saloon" was a male-only refuge, typically closed to view from the street, that protected gambling and prostitution from the scrutiny of wives and women reformers, even as mediocre paintings of naked women lined the walls.[6]

Having looked at many archival photos of establishments identified as saloons, I can report that they share a creepy-basement vibe that would stop me at the threshold should I ever travel back in time. As a historian interested in excavating the various codes—sartorial, slang, gesture—that are used to define the meaning and purpose of public spaces, I lingered over the question of what had provoked this response. It took me a while to realize what seemed so wrong in these photos besides the scuffed floors, dearth of furniture, and gaudy wallpaper. But I eventually figured out that part of the story is not just that these were spaces reserved exclusively for men but that men in these photos are wearing their hats...indoors. What a dramatic rejection of late-century etiquette! Unlike in the cases of male-only colleges, men's athletic clubs, the vibrant adult fraternity scene, the military, or the YMCA, saloon frequenters defined their saloons as spaces wherein the era's rules of polite conduct had been suspended.[7]

Anti-liquor advocates were, of course, focused on more important issues than hat etiquette. They widely decried the fact that once customers were inside a vile saloon, the saloon keeper sought to extract every possible penny from the vulnerably tipsy, profiting the most from the drinkers who became drunkards. Saloons "lured," then "debauched" and "defiled."[8] Consider the free lunch, a saloon staple in the era. Bartenders would offer salty meals, thereby encouraging patrons to buy and drink more alcohol, serving the same purpose that mozzarella sticks and pretzels serve in our own time.[9] Through restrooms, "treating," and entertainment, saloons invited people to stay longer—and in so doing amplified a desire for liquor that might have otherwise abated. The historian Perry Duis documented that Chicago saloons "became almost ubiquitous" as their "ranks grew to the thousands," assuring that "the ratio of people per barroom in Chicago stabilized at 203 to 1 in 1885 and slowly inched downward."[10] Nationwide, the number of saloons was continued to increase; estimates suggest that there was one saloon for every three hundred urban residents, and alcohol consumption seems to have jumped after 1900.[11]

Outraged, ASL leaders nonetheless vowed to carefully moderate their tone, mostly because they wanted to avoid unwittingly producing propaganda that saloon keepers could use to motivate the liquor vote. Consider the example of how the prohibition activist Carrie Nation's destruction of Kansas saloons' bartending fixtures—with an axe, of all things—had cultivated greater sympathy for owners of destroyed saloons.[12] Pro-liquor forces had unified under a legitimate-sounding defense of property rights, opposition to anarchy, and disgust with an unladylike force of nature.[13] If prohibitionists were all like Nation—possessing "an unwelcome air of fanaticism and even burlesque"—why would established politicians and respectable voters take them seriously?[14] Impressed by her dedication but not by her method, ASL leaders insisted that there was no need to take a literal battle axe in hand, when political pressure would do the trick. For example, the *Defender* favorably described an Ohio branch's method of hiring detectives to scout illegal establishments and supply evidence to law-enforcement officers, saying that the action was so efficient that "the result of their efforts in the state during the past year shows up favorably with the Carrie Nation method of putting liquor dealers out of business."[15] The exemplary ASL member was less like Carrie Nation and more like the New York ASL superintendent, William Anderson, an attorney with a law degree from the University of Michigan, a sharp-looking moustache, and a reputation as an incredibly capable professional lobbyist.

ASL leaders also sought to preserve a certain mystique whereby their organization's power appeared virtually unlimited, a task that was easiest if a broad set of anti-liquor benchmarks could count as success.[16] They would not be like the foolish Prohibition Party, which in New York had recently refused to accept the "half loaf" of local option, so that they could not share in the glory when the measure eventually passed.[17] After all, "What is practicable in Brockton, Massachusetts, may be impossible in Peoria, Illinois."[18] Depending upon what seemed likely to succeed, the ASL would support laws to limit the number (or increase the cost) of liquor licenses, make select spirits illegal, assure Sunday closings, promote local option so that counties could develop statutes independently of states, or enact statewide prohibition.[19] As summarized by the historian Thomas Pegram, the ASL would promote "a new temperance sensibility which shunned the antics of Carry Nation and the hopeless crusades of the Prohibition Party."[20]

With consideration of both of these guidelines—that a campaign should never provide the liquor vote with alarmist ammunition and that winnable battles should be preferred to absolutism—the ASL resolved to avoid any legislative coercions that attacked consumption head-on. In what would prove to be an understatement, leaders predicted that restricting personal use would be unpopular.[21] There was "a large section of the great body of men who detest[ed] the grog shop" but felt that anti-consumption statutes would be "sumptuary legislation, and an unwarranted interference with personal liberty." These men's support and donations were needed, and therefore the league would refrain from urging "any legislation looking to the universal suppression of the use of such liquor as beverage."[22] Such legislation would, of course, be very difficult to enforce, and so the ASL warned against them for practical reasons. Better would be legislation following the lead of an early Ohio bill that the ASL praised because "this bill will not restrict any man from drinking," while forcefully forbidding "a *public drinking place* for the private convenience of those who say they can not help drinking." After all, the ASL argued, "it is not necessary to make drunkenness easier."[23]

The ASL's rank-and-file donors seldom had an opportunity to register complaints about how the organization's leadership developed strategy. National conventions were notoriously performative, rather than deliberative, and there were no ASL-affiliated grass-roots organizations complementing the national organization. Nonetheless, there is little to suggest that constituent Methodists, Baptists, and Presbyterians objected to a focus on prohibiting the saloon rather than prohibiting liquor consumption; they definitely disliked the saloon, and religious conventions provided another acceptable outlet for their concerns about sinfulness and their personal sobriety pledges. These donors and voters, moreover, did not shun alliances with drinking or ethically dubious politicians so long as these politicians pursued morally valuable policies.

Sympathy with the drinkers who had made mistakes further assured that anti-saloon advocates did "not press the drinking of alcoholic liquor as a sin *per se*."[24] According to dry advocates, drunkards lost "volition" when alcohol invaded their bodies, a dire description that nonetheless made it possible to imagine prohibition as a precondition for complete redemption and rehabilitation.[25] And by portraying some drinkers as what we would now call "alcoholics," the ASL laid the blame squarely upon the saloon that had enabled these men's self-destruction.[26] In his classic history of the Anti-Saloon League, K. Austin Kerr described how "the officers and supporters of the Anti-Saloon League made no secret of the fact that they were opposed to the consumption of alcoholic beverages, but they consistently emphasized that the means toward their objective of uplifting the individual was the legal destruction of the systems of manufacturing and distributing dangerous beverages."[27]

The saloon was bad in and of itself, argued the Anti-Saloon League, but when resistance to even moderate regulation campaigns emerged, it illuminated a tangled web of political and economic forces.[28] Manufacturers, transportation companies, and wholesalers had rigged the political system to protect their industry, and the ASL publicized struggles to undermine a powerful foe: the liquor traffic. ASL leaders resolved, in the words of the legislative superintendent Wayne Wheeler, that "the only way to clean up the liquor business is to clean it out root and branch."[29]

THE LIQUOR TRAFFIC'S CHALLENGE TO DEMOCRACY, 1869–1893

In deciding to challenge the liquor traffic rather than berate alcohol consumers, and resolving to remove the root (the liquor traffic) to get rid of the branch (the saloon), the ASL relied upon political theory first crafted by the Prohibition Party and the Woman's Christian Temperance Union (WCTU).[30] In the 1870s and 1880s these earlier opponents to the liquor traffic had claimed that close elections and unstable party alignments provided the liquor traffic with tremendous leverage over both Democratic and Republican politicians in the federal government.[31]

Prohibitionists claimed insider knowledge of how the liquor traffic warned politicians that "if either party shall take issue against their business they will leave them."[32] This threat quashed prohibition debates; neither national party would develop a consistent and rigorous national platform that brought the prohibition issue before the people.[33] In Minnesota, dry advocates spotted a parallel "conspiracy of silence" within the state legislature that led to lackluster compromise; both Democratic and Republican representatives agreed to appease dry advocates by raising saloon licensing fees. The cost of licenses could be made so expensive that many saloons would close, but the remaining saloons eagerly paid so as not to suffer under prohibitory rule.[34] The Prohibition Party's founder, John Russell, contended that it was the policy of state legislatures and Congress "to ignore this [prohibition] question as far as possible—to give temperance people just legislation enough to pacify them, and to keep liquor dealers quiet by *not executing* the imperfect statues enacted against their business."[35]

In the liquor traffic and its ostensible control over American politics, dry advocates found an explanation for the hitherto limited success of what they claimed was a wildly popular agenda, namely, prohibition. Seemingly all challenges could be attributed to the liquor traffic's obstructionist work. It was because of the liquor traffic, the WCTU contended, that politicians would not advance women's suffrage resolutions; distillers and brewers were afraid that virtuous women would vote for dry measures and hence threatened to defund politicians who favored enfranchisement.[36] And the complaints of dry men illuminated the extent to which the franchise provided dry voters no sanctuary from liquor-traffic meddling; prohibition-favoring voters had little say in the nominations of over saloon-approved candidates and were locked out of both parties' platform making.[37] For that matter, many election polling places were located within saloons, wherein the saloon keeper controlled access to the ballot box and followed dubious counting practices. In the age of highly visible political bosses and the spoils system, dry advocates perceived the liquor traffic's influence in every bad political practice and policy.

The Prohibition Party had argued that a conspiracy between brewers, distillers, Democrats, and Republicans—an agreement to avoid public debate about prohibition—endured because the federal government also had an autonomous interest in protecting the tax revenue that liquor licenses produced.[38] The ASL chronicler Ernest Cherrington was borrowing from this tradition when he colorfully described how the federal government had been "hushed by the cold bribe of a hundred and eighty million dollar annual federal tax" and had therefore "grown deaf and dumb."[39] Cherrington was here referring to the fact that liquor taxes had historically provided 20–40 percent of federal revenue in most years and would provide 25 percent in 1913. So motivated was the federal government to collect this tax, noted both the WCTU and the Prohibition Party, that it collected it from saloons located in prohibition states.[40]

Even worse, the Prohibition Party claimed, the liquor traffic was taking on the character of that most vile of Progressive Era demons: a trust. Trusts—a category of business that was something between "big business" and "monopoly"—were always suspect because their control of the marketplace made it impossible for new, independent businesses to develop and thereby limited the choices available to consumers.[41] Trusts undermined Americans' independence. The phrase *liquor trust* had grounding in reality. In the 1890s there was a large successful whiskey trust that centralized production. In the same vein, a few national brewers began to dominate beer production, and all brewers moved toward vertically integrated liquor production, distribution, and sales. Typically a brewery would demand an exclusive contract with any saloon selling its product, and every passing year showed fewer breweries and distilleries controlling more and more production and sales.[42] This was the legendary "tied house." When large companies displaced small producers and the owners of independent saloons, entrepreneurs became mere employees. Yet historians also generally agree that *trust* was a misleading term when here applied, given that brewers generally saw distillers as rivals in the beverage market, and vice versa. Hence the liquor business had less harmony of interest than dry advocates seemed to suppose.[43] Assuming the worst rather than observing which conditions actually existed, dry advocates expressed peculiar horror when imagining a trust selling intoxicants. A liquor trust would be a "double threat" because it would undermine people's freedom both economically and corporally, at the same time.[44]

How could a liquor trust's encroachment upon politics be stopped? In my research on the Prohibition Party, I found that prohibitionists consistently argued that only a new major party could attract drys away from the Democrats and Republicans and consolidate these votes, thus forcing the deserted parties to transform themselves into an antiprohibition party.[45] Only the new party system so created could assure that representatives actually held debates about prohibition, thus restoring democracy's capacity to correct social problems through the routine mechanisms of government. The Prohibition Party would be a party for which respectable WCTU women might (someday) vote. It would win elections, argued its advocates, assuring that all new dry laws could be passed with a promise that officeholders would enforce the laws.

As the historian Jack Blocker summarized most concisely, "Party Prohibitionists . . . aimed at neither the salvation of drunkards nor the moral regeneration of society, although they hoped that these would follow in prohibition's train." Rather, "they perceived the liquor traffic as the source of numerous specific social evils including crime, disease, poverty," and most importantly, "political corruption."[46] Throughout most of the 1870s and 1880s the Prohibition Party and the WCTU had argued that purer democracy—organized via a new party system—was the best way to achieve prohibition.[47]

The Anti-Saloon League, in turn, would look at the Prohibition Party's and the WCTU's all-consuming attempts to assemble an organized majority, and how little this work had yielded. Perhaps, pondered ASL leaders, democracy could be restored through prohibition, rather than the other way around. The ASL would develop a balance-of-power strategy according to which a plurality of voters supported or blocked any candidate, regardless of party, based only upon that candidate's opinion regarding prohibition. With politicians under their thumb, the ASL would encourage officeholders to either introduce dry legislation or simply attach anti-liquor amendments to unrelated bills.[48]

About the combination of balance-of-power tactics and the impeccably bureaucratic organizational structure that characterized the ASL, the historian K. Austin Kerr noted that "there was no model to follow, no comparable reform organization."[49] Certainly this approach was quite different from those pursued by the Prohibition Party and the WCTU. So where did it come from? After decades of imagining the phantom of a well-organized and highly influential "liquor traffic," the Tennessee ASL leader Ben Hooper would wryly explain that after all, "this plan is not original. We copied it from the liquor people."[50]

BEATING THE LIQUOR TRAFFIC AT
ITS OWN GAME, 1913–1917

Glancing through a commemorative guide published by the Anti-Saloon League, I spotted a December 1913 photo depicting an enormous crowd of men dressed in winter coats and a smattering of women wearing fancy hats, all standing at attention on the Capitol steps. These one thousand ASL delegates had just delivered to representatives Richmond Hobson (D-AL) and Morris Sheppard (D-TX) a memo containing the ASL's preferred language for a constitutional amendment. Or in the League's words, these delegates had provided the "full text of resolutions delivered to Congress," text that predictably began by urging prohibition of "the sale, manufacture for sale, transportation for sale, and exportation for sale of intoxicating liquors for beverage purposes."[51]

Like virtually all ASL endeavors, this ceremonial transfer was intended to convey the organization's authority; while industrial capitalists, for example, also pressured Congress for prohibitory legislation, they had far less reason to insist upon any particular phrasing of an amendment's language and kept a much lower profile.[52] After the ASL delivered their gift, the delegates entered the building to lobby their representatives and senators.[53] Hobson and Sheppard, together with the ASL delegates, assured that the bill was immediately introduced in both houses and sent to committees. A year later, Hobson would call for a vote from the floor of the House, urging Congress to "destroy the agency that debauches the youth of the land"—the liquor traffic—while remaining silent on the right to consume. "We do not try to force old drinkers to stop drinking," he asserted, just as the ASL had instructed.[54]

The period 1913–17 was one in which the ASL advanced a very risky strategy. Drawing upon the political capital that its reputation as a channeler of popular opinion had generated, the league would press for national prohibition *in advance of* public opinion in hopes of achieving prohibition before a countermovement gained strength.[55] While it's hard to know for sure what motivated the ASL to change up its strategy, an understanding of the organization's political acumen suggests probable reasons: the league's leaders, especially its chief legislative agent at this point, Wayne Wheeler, sensed an opportunity too good to pass up, feared that the liquor traffic was improving its organization, looked anxiously to how the 1920 census might redistribute congressional representation, and desired to misdirect public scrutiny from multiple failed state referendum campaigns—campaigns that had already exposed the limits of the ASL's capacity as a voice for the churches and people.[56] The ASL hoped that without saloons pushing alcohol onto consumers, the remaining alcohol in circulation would be drunk and then quickly forgotten.[57] At the very least, an amendment that rendered alcohol manufacturing illegal might impede this industry's outsized lobbying influence.

The ASL's first attempt at an amendment passed in the Senate but not in the House. Thrilled that the amendment had simply made its way out of committee, the ASL revisited the question of which officeholders could expect a competitive election and decided to wage another campaign almost immediately.[58] The ASL represented, its leaders reminded Congress, a constituency of readers who traced their representatives' careers via *American Issue* and the ASL's other newspapers. Moreover, its supporters had risen high in Congress; for instance, the House Judiciary Committee's chair, Edwin Yates Webb, was a member of the board of directors of the North Carolina ASL.[59]

World War I gave a final push to the long journey. The most notable dry run for the prohibition amendment's big vote was the Lever Food and Fuel Control Act of 1917. The ASL had encouraged members of Congress to attach to this wartime conservation measure a provision banning the processes of turning grain into beverages, which it characterized as wasteful of national resources. Some members of Congress urged their colleagues to expel "these fanatics, hypocrites" who were "talking about the Halls of Congress" and "seeking to stir up hate, envy, jealousy, sectional, racial, and all kinds of animosity" by "trying to influence . . . votes on the amendments pending to the food-control bill."[60]

The ASL provision wound up throwing the bill's passage into jeopardy. To unblock a wartime measure that was splitting both the Democrats and the Republicans along wet-dry lines, President Woodrow Wilson personally wrote to the ASL's legislative committee to request that the league withdraw any objections to a prohibition-free food bill. It was at this point—with a public display in which the president groveled—that a few more senators finally agreed to advance a prohibition amendment, eventually resulting in a favorable vote of 65 to 20.[61] In an awed tone, the temperance orator Ira Landrith described how "the Anti-Saloon League holds the whip-hand in the fight for National Constitutional Prohibition."[62]

Senator Hardwick's exasperated assertion that only statutes against *consumption* would create "complete prohibition, practical prohibition" therefore came at a moment when the ASL was ready for battle and carefully monitoring its alliances. On the one hand, the ASL was pushing and prodding legislators who were not personally abstinent to vote for the amendment; to these individuals, the ASL urged that passing the amendment and sending it to the state legislatures for ratification would not suggest an endorsement of anything other than democracy.[63] On the other hand, many extremely excited dry advocates wanted to take a metaphorical axe in hand and were pushing their legislators for some of the "complete prohibition" that Hardwick offered. Seeking to keep the overly enthusiastic supporters from mucking up ASL negotiations with reluctant legislators, the league promised that keeping consumption legal would make the other parts of the law easier to enforce. The thinking went that the "witness, who, as a rule, is the purchaser" would be more willing to aid in his retailer's conviction if he himself had no fear of prosecution.[64]

In December 1917 the House of Representatives approved the measure by a vote of 282 to 128. State legislatures would in turn ratify the Eighteenth Amendment, temporarily inscribing the prohibition of "manufacture, sale, or transportation of intoxicating liquors within, the importation thereof into, or the exportation thereof from the United States and all territory subject to the jurisdiction thereof for beverage purposes" into the Constitution.

CONCLUSION

The ASL began the twentieth century with a clear and explicit goal: attack the saloon and the liquor traffic that it illuminated. Anti-saloon advocates would tear out by the roots the forces manufacturing, transporting, and selling alcohol, making resurgence as unlikely as possible. This would leave American institutions unencumbered by coercion, able to create policies that served the American people, not the liquor traffic.

So invested were ASL leaders in the idea that the American people would quickly recognize the benefits of national sobriety and recall the drunken age with disdain that a costly battle against consumption seemed like a waste of political power. It would be an unpopular campaign for a goal that could be more easily achieved indirectly. As had been perhaps best predicted by Senator Hardwick's snarky question, the ASL's and Congress's determination to avoid the topic of consumption had consequences. The decision to justify prohibition not as an act for individual moral uplift but instead as a means of extracting the liquor traffic from politics invited a cheeky response: technical accommodation to the law without accepting the spirit in which it was offered. Politicians voting for the prohibition amendment did not ask Americans for moral improvement, so it should not be all that surprising that they didn't get it.

NOTES

1. Thomas Hardwick, Cong. Rec. S5645 (1 August, 1917), italics mine.

2. Jack S. Blocker Jr., *Retreat from Reform: The Prohibition Movement in the United States, 1890–1913* (Westport, CT: Greenwood, 1976), 199–202; K. Austin Kerr, *Organized for Prohibition: A New History of the Anti-Saloon League* (New Haven, CT: Yale University Press, 1985), 99.

3. Ernest Cherrington, *History of the Anti-Saloon League* (Westerville, OH: American Issue, 1913), 74; Harvey Graeme Furbay, "The Anti-Saloon League," *North American Review* 13 (September 1903): 435; Cherrington, *History of the Anti-Saloon League*, 132.

4. Kerr, *Organized for Prohibition;* Blocker, *Retreat from Reform*, 102–4.

5. On the distinction between image and reality, see Perry R. Duis, *The Saloon: Public Drinking in Chicago and Boston, 1880–1920* (Urbana: University of Illinois Press, 1999), 5–6.

6. Andrew Sinclair, *Era of Excess: A Social History of the Prohibition Movement* (New York: Harper & Row, 1962), 231–33; Thomas Pegram, *Battling Demon Rum: Struggle for a Dry America, 1800–1933* (New York: Ivan R. Dee, 1999), 104–5; Duis, *Saloon,* 232.

7. See Clifford Putney, *Muscular Christianity: Manhood and Sports in Protestant America, 1880–1920* (Cambridge, MA: Harvard University Press, 2003); and Mark C. Carnes, *Secret Ritual and Manhood in Victorian America* (New Haven, CT: Yale University Press, 1989). On the etiquette rules for wearing a hat, see http://emilypost.com/advice/hats-off-hat-etiquette-for-everyone/.

8. Louis Albert Banks, "The Boston Tea Party and Carrie Nation," *American Issue* (Columbus, OH) 8 (1 March 1901).

9. For a summary of this custom, see W. J. Rorabaugh, *Prohibition: A Concise History* (New York: Oxford University Press, 2018), 36–38.

10. Duis, *Saloon,* 8, 28.

11. Michael Lewis, "Access to Saloons, Wet Voter Turnout, and Statewide Prohibition Referenda, 1907–1919," *Social Science History* 32 (Fall 2008); Kerr, *Organized for Prohibition;* Pegram, *Battling Demon Rum,* 91–92. See also Norman Clarke, *Deliver Us from Evil* (New York: Norton, 1976), cited in Pegram, *Battling Demon Rum,* 96.

12. "John Brown and Carrie Nation," *American Issue* (Columbus, OH) 8 (15 February 1901); W. F. Macauley, "The Nation versus the Saloon," *American Issue* 8 (1 March 1901).

13. Elaine Franz Parsons, *Manhood Lost: Fallen Drunkards and Redeeming Women in the Nineteenth-Century United States* (Baltimore: Johns Hopkins University Press, 2010), 178–81.

14. Pegram, *Battling Demon Rum,* 111.

15. *The Defender,* quoted in "Anti-Saloon Work in Adams County," *American Issue* 8 (1 March 1901).

16. Kerr, *Organized for Prohibition,* 196–97, 209; Jack S. Blocker Jr., *American Temperance Movements: Cycles of Reform* (Boston: Twayne, 1989), 104–5.

17. "A Prohibition Journal on Local Option," *American Issue,* April 1900, reprinted from the *New Standard* (Birmingham, NY). See also Blocker, *Retreat from Reform,* 164.

18. Furbay, "Anti-Saloon League," 435. Peoria was the distilling center of the nation.

19. Blocker, *American Temperance Movements,* 104.

20. Pegram, *Battling Demon Rum,* 112.

21. Richard F. Hamm, *Shaping the Eighteenth Amendment: Temperance Reform, Legal Culture, and the Polity, 1880–1920* (Chapel Hill: University of North Carolina Press, 1995), 223; Michael A. Lerner, *Dry Manhattan: Prohibition in New York City* (Cambridge, MA: Harvard University Press, 2007), 45.

22. Herrick Johnson, "Principle and Method in the Temperance Reform," *Anti-Saloon,* October 1894.

23. David O. Mears, "An Eloquent Plea" (excerpt of Hearing at House Committee on Temperance), *Anti-Saloon,* March 1894, italics mine.

The Prohibition Amendment Sought to Ban Individual Drinking   51

24. Johnson, "Principle and Method in the Temperance Reform."

25. Parsons, *Manhood Lost,* 130.

26. Sabine N. Meyer, *We Are What We Drink: The Temperance Battle in Minnesota* (Urbana: University of Illinois Press, 2015), 126.

27. Kerr, *Organized for Prohibition,* 3.

28. Pegram, "The Dry Machine: The Formation of the Anti-Saloon League of Illinois," *Illinois Historical Journal* 83 (Autumn 1990): 175.

29. *Proceedings of the Fifteenth National Convention of the Anti-Saloon League of America* (Westerville, OH: American Issue, 1913), 17.

30. Blocker, *American Temperance Movements,* 99–102.

31. See Ann-Marie E. Szymanski, *Pathways to Prohibition: Radicals, Moderates, and Social Movement Outcomes* (Durham, NC: Duke University Press, 2003), 13; and Lisa M. F. Andersen, *Politics of Prohibition: American Governance and the Prohibition Party, 1869–1933* (New York: Cambridge University Press, 2013), 30, 38–40.

32. State Central Committee of the Temperance Party of Michigan, "Address," *Peninsular Herald,* 3 March 1869.

33. Andersen, *Politics of Prohibition,* 43–44.

34. Meyer, *We Are What We Drink,* 94–99, 137.

35. John Russell, *An Adequate Remedy for a National Evil* (Detroit: New World Book and Job Print, 1872), 6, italics original.

36. Ruth Bordin, *Woman and Temperance: The Quest for Power and Liberty, 1783–1900* (New Brunswick, NJ: Rutgers University Press, 1990), 118–99; Meyer, *We Are What We Drink,* 89–91; Andersen, *Politics of Prohibition,* 62–95.

37. Andersen, *Politics of Prohibition,* 37–40, 111–13.

38. Andersen, *Politics of Prohibition* 14–15, 57–58, 153–54.

39. Cherrington, *History of the Anti-Saloon League,* 8; Office of Management and Government, "Fiscal Year 2016: Historical Tables" accessed January 2019, https://www.govinfo.gov/content/pkg/BUDGET-2016-TAB/pdf/BUDGET-2016-TAB.pdf. Earlier in US States history, liquor taxes had provided as much as one-half of federal revenue. Blocker, *American Temperance Movements,* 66.

40. Hamm, *Shaping the Eighteenth Amendment,* 95–96, 156–57.

41. Robyn Munch, "Trustbusting and White Manhood in America," *American Studies* 38 (Fall 1997): 25.

42. Pegram, *Battling Demon Rum,* 93–96; Blocker, *American Temperance Movements,* 65–66; Duis, *Saloon,* 15, 21–29, 36–40; Kerr, *Organized for Prohibition,* 14–15.

43. On the alcohol industry's actual disunity, see Hamm, *Shaping the Eighteenth Amendment,* 44–48. On the ASL picking up this line of thinking, see Lerner, *Dry Manhattan,* 23; and Pegram, *Battling Demon Rum,* 100–101.

44. Pegram, *Battling Demon Rum,* 101.

45. Andersen, *Politics of Prohibition,* esp. 30. See also Blocker, *Retreat from Reform,* 39–41.

46. Blocker, *American Temperance Movements*, 86–87.

47. Andersen, *Politics of Prohibition*, 27.

48. Blocker, *Retreat from Reform*, 162; Kerr, *Organized for Prohibition*, 131.

49. Kerr, *Organized for Prohibition*, 90.

50. *Proceedings of the Fifteenth National Convention*, 33.

51. Anti-Saloon League of America, *The Battle for National Prohibition* (Westerville, OH: American Issue, [1914?]). See also Rorabaugh, *Prohibition*, 54.

52. On capitalists, see John Rumbarger, *Profits, Power, and Prohibition: Alcohol Reform and the Industrializing of America, 1800–1930* (Albany: State University of New York Press, 1989). On the ASL and business alliances, see Kerr, *Organized for Prohibition*, 154.

53. Ernest Cherrington, ed., *Anti-Saloon League of America Year Book for 1914* (Westerville, OH: American Issue, 1914), 7.

54. Cong. Rec., 22 December 1914, cited in Kerr, *Organized for Prohibition*, 1.

55. Blocker, *Retreat from Reform*, 229; Kerr, *Organized for Prohibition*, 141.

56. Blocker, *American Temperance Movements*, 112–13; Blocker, *Retreat from Reform*, 214–22.

57. Catherine Gilbert Murdock, *Domesticating Drink: Women, Men, and Alcohol in America, 1870–1940* (Baltimore: Johns Hopkins University Press, 1998), 90; Kerr, *Organized for Prohibition*, 13.

58. Wayne Wheeler, in *Proceedings of the Anti-Saloon League of America, National Convention of 1917* (Westerville, OH: American Issue, 1917), 75.

59. Kerr, *Organized for Prohibition*, 195.

60. Leonidas Dyer, Cong. Rec. H5529–30 (26 July 1917).

61. James Cannon Jr., in *Proceedings of the National Convention* (1917), 155–56.

62. *Proceedings of the National Convention* (1917), 57.

63. Kerr, *Organized for Prohibition*, 194.

64. George Norris, Cong. Rec. S5645 (1 August 1917).

MYTH 4

PROHIBITION IN THE UNITED STATES CAME ABOUT PRIMARILY BECAUSE OF WORLD WAR I

ANN-MARIE E. SZYMANSKI

When prohibition went into effect on January 16, 1920, it had no impact on my husband's great-grandparents, Lewis and Mary Gatch, of Milford, Ohio. Devout Methodists, the Gatches never drank and maintained a dry household.[1] Lewis and Mary were not alone; many Americans had banished alcoholic beverages from their lives years before prohibition was adopted. They were also like millions of other Americans who already knew what it was like to live in a community that had banned the sale and manufacture of alcoholic beverages before 1920. As residents of Milford, the Gatches watched as their town voted "wet" (to retain its saloons) in 1904 but then voted "dry" in 1908 and 1913, when Clermont County voters had the opportunity to decide the liquor question, thus suppressing the town's two saloons.[2] They also witnessed the proposal of four statewide ballot measures (1914, 1915, 1917, and 1918) designed to incorporate prohibition into the Ohio state constitution and the vigorous campaigns between wets and drys that arose in the wake of these proposed referenda.[3] Given this lengthy prologue, prohibition was less a sharp break with the past and more an expansion of anti-liquor policies that millions of Americans had debated, considered, and cast ballots for and against during the Progressive Era (1900–1920).

Historians have often suggested that America's entry into World War I in April 1917 significantly increased the support for prohibition among political elites and the broader public.[4] To bolster this argument, they note that the wartime government set the stage for national prohibition when it dramatically increased its intervention in the national economy, thus lending legitimacy to a nationwide anti-liquor policy that otherwise might have raised stronger opposition from states' rights supporters than it did. Likewise, scholars point out that anti-liquor activists were able to capitalize on the federal government's emergency powers to secure wartime prohibition. For example, they limited liquor production for the purposes of food conservation by keeping grain from being made into alcohol, and this underscored dry claims that prohibition was patriotic. Finally, they observe that during World War I the national government disseminated anti-German propaganda, which invariably weakened the political power of wet groups like the German-American Alliance (GAA) and German American brewers, the latter of whom had assembled the best-funded anti-prohibition organization. Indeed, they contend that anti-liquor activists profited greatly from the 1916 revelations that the GAA had supported the German war effort since 1914, as well as the February 1918 Senate hearings which revealed that the United States Brewers' Association (USBA) had bankrolled the GAA and wet newspaper content, therefore discrediting the USBA just as the states began ratifying the Eighteenth Amendment in 1918.

While certainly accelerated by the wartime atmosphere, national prohibition was not the product of a sudden burst of patriotic fervor or the rapid growth of the federal government after the war began. Rather, the adoption of the Eighteenth Amendment was the culmination of a lengthy process in which anti-liquor forces sponsored local, county, and state contests that highlighted the saloon's ostensibly harmful impact on families, the social order, and the economy. As the leading anti-liquor organization after 1900, the Anti-Saloon League (ASL) viewed this approach as practical, educational, and an opportunity to mobilize citizens for policies that could reduce the number of saloons in their states and communities. As the twentieth century progressed, the ASL further benefited from the growing legitimacy of constitutional change as a solution to a wide range of political problems, including the liquor question.

ANTI-LIQUOR ACTIVISM AT THE LOCAL LEVEL

To marshal grass-roots support for prohibition, the ASL systematically developed vehicles for local agitation. First, it hoped to supplement the states' existing prohibitory measures with modest laws that advanced the drys' position vis-à-vis the wets'. In northern states like Ohio, where the extant local option system was typically limited, the league sought to extend and improve on that system so as to facilitate more effective local activism. After 1900, the Ohio league secured legislative support for the municipal option (1902), the residence-district option (1906), and the county option (1908), policies that allowed voters of an established geographical region to decide whether to license saloons in their locality.[5] Meanwhile, in the South, with its well-developed local option laws, the ASL tended to focus on achieving statewide measures that established prohibition in the rural areas. If successful, such state legislative campaigns helped the league to consolidate and add to the amount of dry territory in the nation as a whole.[6] However, even if their legislative proposals faltered, ASL leaders recognized, these campaigns would be beneficial to the prohibition movement in other ways. In 1903, for example, William H. Anderson made the following arguments in favor of a crusade for local option in Illinois: "The indirect benefits of the passage of the bill will be greater than the direct ones.... The important thing will be the aroused, organized public sentiment that will make it possible. It affords a tangible concrete rallying-point. It will impress men with the practicability of temperance work, and prepare them to follow intelligent leadership in the next step. But best of all, it will allow us to force upon the liquor men an issue of our own choosing, whether majority rule shall be perpetuated in this state or go down in shame before an oligarchy of brewers."[7]

In either case, the ASL inevitably adapted to each state's unique legal situation to exploit whatever tools were available to press its cause at the local level. As in Ohio, most state leagues relied on some kind of local option. In other states, however, the path forward was less clear-cut. In South Carolina, for example, anti-liquor activists had no choice but to adjust to the dispensary system developed in 1893 by Governor Ben Tillman, which replaced barrooms with state-run liquor stores. Only after South Carolinians became more familiar with the flaws and corruption of the state dispensary system were anti-liquor forces able to secure support for a 1904 local option law, the Bryce law, which empowered the counties to vote out their state-run retail liquor stores through referenda.[8] Meanwhile, in Pennsylvania anti-liquor activists found themselves exploiting the Byzantine provisions of the Brooks Law (1887) for the duration of the Progressive Era. According to that law, the judges of the local courts of quarter sessions had sole authority to determine how many applicants, if any, should be granted retail liquor licenses. Before deciding, the judges were required to examine all remonstrances for and against license applications. Consequently, the drys decided to make a systematic effort to elect sympathetic judges and to circulate remonstrances against license applicants.[9]

Like the campaigns for modest state prohibitory laws, locally based efforts proved to be of great value to the prohibition movement. Obviously, the ASL sponsored local campaigns in order to drive the liquor traffic out of as many villages, towns, and counties as it could, but that was hardly their only purpose. For league leaders, the outcomes of these local campaigns were a rough indication of the strength and weakness of anti-liquor sentiment at the state and local levels. Furthermore, anti-liquor contests demonstrated the extent of the ASL's influence and informed public officials of their constituents' preferences on the liquor issue. In legislative debates, lawmakers often used local option results to discuss their constituents' views on this subject. For example, state sen-

ator William S. Alee of Miller County, Missouri, noted that he was unde-
cided about whether he would vote to submit a prohibition amendment
to the voters of his state, because his district included "three 'dry' and
three 'wet' counties."[10] Finally, as the league itself argued, "The greatest
service of [a locally based] system consists in its creation of public sentiment in the various communities of the state by bringing the question
directly before the people and compelling its thoughtful consideration
at the hands of the citizens engaged in all pursuits."[11]

Indeed, ASL leaders only sponsored state prohibition campaigns after they sensed that a state's public opinion favored such a policy. In
some cases, such as the failed Michigan campaign of 1912–13, they over-
estimated their capacity to organize a state prohibition campaign and
had to retreat to a less advanced position.[12] In other states, the league
knew that a state prohibition campaign would be futile and refused to
sponsor one. For instance, when the Illinois Prohibition Party appeared
ready to push for state prohibition in 1910, the state ASL was well aware
of the movement's weakness in Chicago and opposed the plan. "We believe it would be a foolish blunder to bring on a statewide vote," one
league leader declared, "and we are hoping the friends of local option
will see the wisdom of striving for something that is possible instead of
something that is impossible."[13] But once the ASL thought state prohibition was possible, its leaders drew upon their carefully cultivated base
of mass support to fight for the policy. By December 18, 1917, the day
Congress officially proposed a national prohibition amendment to the
US Constitution, twenty-three states maintained some form of statewide prohibition.

Ultimately, league leaders chose their battles carefully after 1900.
Instead of expending scarce resources on securing referenda in states
that were unlikely to vote dry, movement leaders focused on building up
as much support for prohibition as they could in "hopelessly wet" states
like New York and Wisconsin through local option laws. Such a strategy
proved wise, as the ASL would need the support of thirty-six states to
ratify a national prohibition amendment to the US Constitution, and
even the "hopelessly wet" states were governed by legislatures that pro-

vided disproportionate representation to the rural populations that were most amenable to prohibition. Significantly, league leaders were well aware of their advantages in rural America, and they viewed the political terrain as more favorable for prohibition in a political system that relied on the 1910 census for determining representation than one based on the upcoming 1920 census, which would reflect the nation's growing population of wet immigrants in its burgeoning cities. Not surprisingly, then, their campaign for a national prohibition amendment began in 1913.[14] However, the timing of their national-amendment campaign was also based on other factors, such as an upsurge in campaigns for constitutional change that sought to overcome the traditional limits on the national government's power.

AN UPSURGE IN CONSTITUTIONAL CHANGE

To achieve prohibition on a national basis, most anti-liquor activists acknowledged that a constitutional amendment would be necessary given the existing understanding of federal power under the Constitution. For the first hundred years of American history, jurists, public officials, and other political actors viewed the federal government as limited by its enumerated powers under the US Constitution. The federal government could exercise police power—the power to legislate concerning the safety, health, morals, and general welfare of the people—in those small territories (e.g., the District of Columbia) where the Constitution granted it direct control, but for the most part, it was the state governments, bolstered by the Tenth Amendment, that possessed this broad expanse of unlimited authority, which could serve as the basis of regulatory power within state boundaries. Moreover, the federal courts enhanced the states' claim to such power after the Civil War when they issued a series of rulings that held that the federal government could not impose its will on intrastate commerce, for that remained the dominion of the state governments.[15] While a growing number of federal laws suggested that the national government possessed some kind of police power after 1885,[16] they were more useful to the prohibition movement in its quest to secure congressional approval in 1913 of the Webb-Kenyon Act, which provided federal support for state policies that banned the importation of alcohol into any state for use contrary to state law. Upheld by the US Supreme Court in *James Clark Distilling Co. v. Western Maryland R. Co.* (1917), a case personally argued by the ASL leader Wayne Wheeler, this law encouraged a new wave of anti-liquor activity in the states, but it primarily enhanced the police power of the states rather than that of the federal government.[17] To obtain a direct role for the federal government in suppressing the sale and manufacture of alcoholic beverages, then, the drys would need to secure an amendment to the US Constitution.

Anti-liquor activists had first proposed that prohibition should be enshrined in the US Constitution during the 1870s, in the wake of the adoption of the Thirteenth, Fourteenth, and Fifteenth Amendments. In 1876, the Prohibition Party called for a national constitutional amendment to make prohibition both "universal and permanent."[18] However, during the late nineteenth century prohibitionists focused primarily on amending state constitutions, which was viewed as legitimate since many of these documents already included clauses that were extraneous to the government's basic framework.[19] It was only in December 1913 that the ASL and its allies announced a campaign to seek a national constitutional amendment. This new push for a national amendment came in the wake of successful ratification campaigns for two other constitutional amendments: the Sixteenth, which authorized the enactment of the income tax, and the Seventeenth, which authorized direct election of senators. In fact, anti-liquor activists launched their amendment campaign during a period in which "constitutional change was thought of and pursued as a solution to a number of major political problems."[20]

After the triumphant campaigns for the Sixteenth and Seventeenth Amendments, many observers concluded that the amendment process offered the citizenry "an easy, simple remedy" to achieve national goals that might otherwise be subject to constitutional scrutiny or nullification by the US Supreme Court.[21] Some social movements came to view the amendment process as a back-up plan should their preferred statutes be invalidated by the federal judiciary. Concerned that the Supreme Court would strike down the Weeks-McClean Act (1913) and its attempt to impose national control over the hunting of migratory birds, several wildlife activists concluded that a constitutional amendment might be necessary to sustain such a regulatory regime. "While we have every hope that the Supreme Court of the United States will hold the law to be constitutional," opined *Forest and Stream* in 1915, "we suggest that no harm will be done if [wildlife advocates] ... shall begin preparation for the necessity of such an amendment to the Constitution ..., immediately after the decision of the Supreme Court shall have been announced and assuming it is to be negative."[22] Meanwhile, old ideas found new life. On January 24, 1914, Frederick Gillett (R-MA) introduced a long-discussed anti-polygamy amendment in the House of Representatives, and the National Reform Association scheduled a series of mass meetings and petition drives to drum up support for it.[23] Likewise, the campaigns for amendments to secure women's suffrage and prohibition revived long-cherished goals, and they were well positioned to capitalize on the new legitimacy of constitutional change.[24]

THE ADOPTION OF THE FEDERAL INCOME TAX

This new era of constitutional change also had more practical consequences for the proposal of a national prohibition amendment. Beginning in 1862, the alcohol excise tax served as a significant source of federal tax revenue for decades and helped finance the Civil War, veterans' pensions, and the Spanish-American War. A national prohibition amendment would deprive the government of more than 30 percent (on average) of its annual revenue, thus raising the question how such revenue could be replaced.[25] As mentioned previously, the campaign for the Sixteenth Amendment, which authorized the enactment of a national income tax, succeeded in securing ratification from three-fourths of the states in 1913. (In fact, many members of Congress who supported the federal income tax also voted to submit the national prohibition amendment.) The subsequent congressional adoption of a federal-income-tax law in 1913 weakened the wet argument that prohibition would significantly reduce federal tax revenues. "How Can U.S. Make Up the $225,000,000 Taxes that Will Be Lost When the Entire Nation is Drier than Sahara?" queried one widely circulated article. The author of this article noted that the "organized opposition to the saloon" provided an answer to this question by noting that "our income tax law is a mere beginning in taxing incomes. A moderate increase in the rate of taxation on the higher incomes would yield without any difficulty all the money lost by abolishing the liquor traffic."[26]

DISARRAY IN THE OPPOSITION TO PROHIBITION

Of course, many historical developments contributed to the deteriorating influence of the opposition to prohibition as of 1918, including World War I. Certainly, the ASL and its allies exploited anti-German sentiment to discredit their opponents and to associate their cause with the patriotic "war to end all wars." However, the wets had steadily lost ground prior to the war and had long presented a divided front in response to the anti-liquor movement. Convinced that the distribution system was responsible for much of the public's animus toward the liquor industry, the distillers mounted a campaign in 1908 for the creation of model license laws and model saloons, which would shut down barrooms that accommodated prostitution and gambling and refused to limit their hours of operation. Meanwhile, the brewers tried to convince the public that beer, because of its relatively low alcohol content, was a temperance drink. Neither of these public-relations efforts bore much fruit. Despite the drive for model saloons, many liquor retailers continued to welcome unsavory activities and to ignore legal limits on their hours and operations. Likewise, the relative virtues of beer could not hide the fact that the brewing industry bankrolled the saloons and engaged in bribery and other dubious activities to help them flourish.[27]

In the end, World War I may have harmed the cause of prohibition more than it helped it. Lewis and Mary Gatch may have retained their dry lifestyle after 1920, but their oldest son, John, did not. Like many other young Americans of this period, Lieutenant John N. Gatch expanded his social and cultural horizons during the war effort.[28] While stationed in Paris, a place where alcoholic beverages were both ubiquitous and respectable, Lieutenant Gatch met Orpha Gerrans, a Red Cross volunteer and the daughter of a prominent Buffalo hotelier who maintained elegant barrooms in his various hotels. During their whirlwind romance, John and Orpha enjoyed wine at restaurants and champagne after their wedding in St. Nazaire, France, on February 8, 1919. When they returned to the United States in June 1919, wartime prohibition was about to go into effect. Met by family members at the pier in New York city, the newlyweds were soon on their way to a celebratory luncheon at the Hotel McAlpin. When asked what he wanted to drink, John replied, "One dry martini." As Orpha recalled, "Mother and father Gatch had never seen their boys touch liquor. . . . I was proud of him. That was the first time his parents had ever seen him drink." A new generation of Americans saw drinking as both reputable and enjoyable, and the dry attitudes of the elder Gatches were soon to be a relic of the past.[29]

NOTES

1. Orpha Gerrans Gatch, *Memoirs of Orpha Gerrans Gatch,* ed. David Randall Boone (Cincinnati, OH, 1992), 129–30. In fact, the Gatches were so devout that they did not take the Sunday newspaper, prompting their two sons to visit a friend to read the Sunday comics.

2. "Lively Local Option Election," *Cincinnati Enquirer,* 4 August 1904, 12; "Brannock's Home Goes 'Wet,'" *Perrysburg Journal,* 12 August 1904, 7; "Batavia, Nov. 23," *Democrat-Sentinel,* 26 November 1908, 1; "Clermont County Goes Dry," *News-Herald,* 2 October 1913, 1.

3. K. Austin Kerr, *Organized for Prohibition: A New History of the Anti-Saloon League* (New Haven, CT: Yale University Press, 1985), 169–72.

4. For variants of this argument, see Daniel Okrent, *Last Call: The Rise and Fall of Prohibition* (New York: Scribner, 2010), 97–103; Thomas R. Pegram, *Battling Demon Rum: The Struggle for a Dry America, 1800–1933* (Chicago: Ivan R. Dee, 1999), 144–48; Andrew Sinclair, *Prohibition: The Era of Excess* (Boston: Little, Brown, 1962), 119–21; and Charles Merz, *The Dry Decade* (Garden City, NY: Doubleday, Doran, 1931), 25–42.

5. Kerr, *Organized for Prohibition,* chap. 4.

6. Ann-Marie Szymanski, "Beyond Parochialism: Southern Progressivism, Prohibition, and State Building," *Journal of Southern History* 69 (February 2003): 110–22.

7. William H. Anderson, "The Need of Illinois," *American Issue* 10 (23 January 1903): 3.

8. Michael Lewis, *The Coming of Southern Prohibition: The Dispensary System and the Battle over Liquor in South Carolina, 1907–1915* (Baton Rouge: Louisiana State University Press, 2016), 11–94.

9. Ann-Marie Szymanski, *Pathways to Prohibition: Radicals, Moderates, and Social Movement Outcomes* (Durham, NC: Duke University Press, 2003), 168–69.

10. "Law Makers Favor State Vote; Few Want Prohibition," *St. Louis Post-Dispatch*, 11 April 1909, 25.

11. Ernest H. Cherrington, *The Anti-Saloon Yearbook, 1909* (Columbus, OH: Anti-Saloon League of America, 1909), 168.

12. In Michigan, the prohibitionists needed to collect about fifty thousand signatures from voters to place their prohibition amendment on the ballot, but they failed to do so by the fall of 2013. See Larry D. Engelmann, "Oh Whiskey: The History of Prohibition in Michigan" (PhD diss., University of Michigan, 1971), 199–200, 221.

13. "Liquor's Foes Are Divided: Anti-Saloon Men Will Not Support State Wide Prohibition," *Chicago Tribune*, 19 April 1910, 4.

14. Kerr, *Organized for Prohibition*, 187–92; Okrent, *Last Call*, 80–81, 104–6.

15. Walter Wheeler Cook, "What Is the Police Power?" *Columbia Law Review* 7 (1907): 322–36; *U.S. v. DeWitt*, 76 U.S. (9 Wall) 41 (1869); *U.S. v. E. C. Knight Co.*, 156 U.S. 1 (1895).

16. Such measures included the Indian Intermarriage Act (1888), the Anti-Lottery Act (1895), the Oleomargarine Acts (1896), the Mann Act (1910), and the White Phosphorus Match Act (1912). See R. Alton Lee, "The Eradication of Phossy Jaw: A Unique Development of Federal Police Power," *Historian* 29 (November 1966): 1–28; and Kathleen S. Sullivan, "Marriage and Federal Police Power," *Studies in American Political Development* 20 (2006): 45–56.

17. Richard Hamm, *Shaping the Eighteenth Amendment: Temperance, Legal Culture, and the Polity* (Chapel Hill: University of North Carolina Press, 1995), 213–20. The Webb-Kenyon Act's adherence to a states'-rights framework was echoed in contemporary press coverage. For example, the *New York World* opined when the Supreme Court upheld the Webb-Kenyon Act, "It has given to the doctrine of state rights a new force and a new direction." See "An Epoch-Making Decision," editorial, *New York World*, [ca. January 1917], quoted in *Reidsville (NC) Review*, 12 January 1917, 4; *LaFayette (AL) Sun*, 17 January 1917, 6; and *Daily Ardmoreite* (Ardmore, OK), 18 January 1917, 4.

18. D. Leigh Colvin, *Prohibition in the United States* (New York: George H. Doran, 1926), 109–10.

19. Szymanski, *Pathways to Prohibition*, 97–100. Among other things, state constitutions included provisions that banned lotteries, betting at elections, and the promise of

money to voters, as well as provisions that authorized state governments to regulate railroads, warehouses, and grain elevators.

20. David E. Kyvig, *Explicit and Authentic Acts: Amending the U.S. Constitution, 1776–2005* (Lawrence: University Press of Kansas, 2016), chap. 9.

21. James McDonough, "Amending the Constitutional Amendment of the United States," *Central Law Journal* 76 (1913): 335–41; Joseph R. Long, "Tinkering with the Constitution," *Yale Law Journal* 24 (1914–15): 586–87.

22. "Protecting Migratory Birds," *Forest and Stream,* September 1915, 544. See also the following from *Forest and Stream:* Sydney G. Fisher, "An Open Letter to Congressman Lacey," 30 June 1906, 1032; "Conservation in New York State," 27 December 1913; Herbert K. Job, "The Problem of the Wildfowl," 21 February 1914, 240; and "Address of Senator George P. McClean," 24 October 1914, 528. In the end, wildlife advocates and public officials were able to repackage the Weeks-McClean Act as a treaty, the Migratory Bird Treaty, which was upheld by the Supreme Court in *Missouri v. Holland* (1920). See Ann-Marie Szymanski, "Wildlife Protection and the Development of Centralized Governance in the Progressive Era," in *Statebuilding from the Margins: Between Reconstruction and the New Deal,* ed. Carol Nackenoff and Julie Novkov (Philadelphia: University of Pennsylvania Press, 2014), 162–70.

23. Joan Iversen, *The Antipolygamy Controversy in U.S. Women's Movements, 1880–1925: A Debate on the American Home* (New York: Routledge, 1997), 244–45; Patrick Q. Nelson, "Opposition to Polygamy in the South," *Journal of Southern History* 76 (August 2010): 571–73.

24. Kyvig, *Explicit and Authentic Acts,* chap. 10.

25. Hamm, *Shaping the Eighteenth Amendment,* chap. 3.

26. Okrent, *Last Call,* 53–59; "How Can U.S. Make Up the $225,000,000 Taxes that Will Be Lost When the Entire Nation is Drier than Sahara?.," *Muskogee Times-Democrat,* 15 April 1915, 1, 12. Other newspapers published this article under different titles. See, e.g., "Looking for New Tax Sources in Case the Nation Goes Dry," *St. Mary's Beacon* (Leonard Town, MD), 6 May 1915, 2; "What of the Lost Revenue?," *Kansas City Globe,* 20 May 1915, 4; and "What of the Lost Revenue?," *Kansas City (KS) Weekly Gazette Globe,* 15 July 1915, 3.

27. Kerr, *Organized for Prohibition,* chap. 7.

28. See, e.g., "Keep Chief of Army Police Busy," *Dixon (IL) Evening Telegraph,* 26 June 1918, 2.

29. Gatch, *Memoirs of Orpha Gerrans Gatch,* 1–129.

MYTH 5

ALCOHOL CONSUMPTION INCREASED DURING THE PROHIBITION ERA

MICHAEL LEWIS

When I tell people that my research examines prohibition, their first response is almost always to share a story about a relative who drank during the prohibition era, usually in some clandestine and mildly dangerous setting. As it happens, I too have a family prohibition story. It takes place in 1929 in New York City, where my grandfather had a job as a delivery boy. Though the details changed slightly through his many retellings, the essentials are as follows: "One day I was asked to bring a very large crate and some letters to City Hall. The letters I left with the mayor's secretary, but she told me to bring the crate directly into the mayor's office. When she opened the door, there was Mayor Jimmy Walker! He looked at the package, shook my hand and thanked me, and then, before I had a chance to leave, opened the crate. Inside were more bottles of alcohol than I had ever seen. Mayor Walker reached in, grabbed a bottle, and offered it to me. But you know I'm such a square that I just said 'no thank you' and went on my way."

I must confess that I have no idea whether this story is entirely (or even mostly) accurate. Given how little time Mayor Walker was reputed to have spent at City Hall, it does seem just a bit coincidental.[1] Regardless, it serves as a good example of the larger point such tales make, namely, that prohibition did little or nothing to curb the flow of (or appetite for) liquor. Further, if every family has stories that feature the unrestricted flow of alcohol, then that must mean lots of folks drank during prohibition.

What historians tell us about the prohibition law would seem to confirm this conclusion.[2] The dry law permitted physicians, druggists, and manufacturers of proprietary medicines to prescribe and distribute liquor for medicinal purposes as long as they had a license to do so. The production of near beer was still legal, as was the production of industrial alcohol. Further, the federal government took on quite an impossible enforcement task when it adopted prohibition, as all of America's lengthy borders, home producers, and small-scale producers of alcohol would need to be monitored if the law was to have its intended effect. Alongside these enforcement difficulties, it is likely that for some individuals prohibition created a "forbidden fruit effect," drawing people to drink precisely because it had the air of illegality, danger, and excitement without being overly risky. Taken together, these factors make it reasonable to argue that prohibition would have had little chance of reducing alcohol consumption.

Although such conclusions seem obvious, it is important to remember that alongside people like Mayor Walker, who openly flouted the law, were folks like my grandfather, who refused to join them. Some of this refusal was the direct result of the prohibition law. For consumers, prohibition reduced easy access to sellers (perhaps the reason behind my grandfather's surprise at the amount of alcohol he had just delivered to the mayor's office). For producers, prohibition increased the costs necessary to make and sell liquor by adding to the usual production value the need to evade detection and the potential cost of punishment, all of which necessitated higher prices.[3] Looking beyond economic forces, prohibition was enacted at least in part due to a prevailing sentiment that intemperance was harmful and that for many potential drinkers (like my grandfather, a self-proclaimed "square") engaging in an activity that knowingly abetted criminals was too great a line to cross. Taken together, these factors make it reasonable to argue that prohibition did in fact lower alcohol consumption.

My goal in this essay, then, is to look beyond family stories and use statistical evidence to take the measure of the prohibition law and its impact on drinking. Put simply, our question is, what impact did prohibition have on alcohol consumption?

The greatest limitation to answering this question is the lack of data on alcohol consumption during prohibition. Once alcohol sales were made illegal, records of those sales activities were also pushed underground, so there is no hard evidence detailing how much liquor was produced or sold. One way around this void is to compare rates of legal consumption in the years immediately before and after prohibition. We can also examine rates of two proxies related to alcohol consumption: cirrhosis of the liver and arrests for drunkenness.

The definitive source for legal-consumption rates is the yearly surveillance reports published by the National Institute of Alcohol Abuse and Alcoholism (NIAAA). Comparative data on per capita ethanol consumption clearly show that legal consumption was higher from 1916 to 1919 (1.96 gallons) than in 1935 (1.20 gallons). Although this is not direct evidence of consumption patterns during the prohibition era, it certainly suggests that the law did lower consumption.

Of the two proxies for alcohol consumption during prohibition, the majority of researchers opt to use rates of deaths resulting from cirrhosis. Extensive biomedical evidence has confirmed that alcohol consumption causes by far the greater number of deaths related to cirrhosis than other factors.[4] But because cirrhosis is closely associated with heavy alcohol consumption, relying on rates of deaths from cirrhosis undoubtedly undercounts those who drink sparingly. Most researchers accept this limitation, reasoning that heavy drinkers are likely to be responsible for the majority of alcohol consumption; nonetheless, this proxy is not a complete measure of all who drank.

Data on cirrhosis death rates are gathered annually by the NIAAA and tabulated as the rate of deaths per one hundred thousand people, adjusted for the age distribution of the population (to account for the fact that the majority of cirrhosis deaths occur after age thirty-five).[5] Since higher cirrhosis death rates are known to be strongly correlated with higher alcohol consumption, the simplest way researchers can assess prohibition's impact is to compare cirrhosis death rates before and after prohibition with those during the prohibition era. The table below shows these data beginning in 1914, six years before federal prohibition, through 1935, three years after repeal. The table shows a dramatic decline in the years leading up to federal prohibition, followed by a smaller drop toward the end of the prohibition era. Taken as a whole, these results support the assertion that alcohol consumption was lower during the prohibition era than in the years before the federal law was enacted. Further strengthening the correlation between prohibition and cirrhosis is the ten-year lag period that medical researchers agree needs to be factored in to account for the time cirrhosis takes to have its full impact. So, if prohibition in 1920 did lower alcohol consumption, then its impact should have begun to make itself felt toward the end of the decade, which is exactly what the cirrhosis rates show. Based on this simple comparison, we would conclude that prohibition reduced cirrhosis and therefore alcohol consumption.[6]

Rates of Death from Cirrhosis and Arrests for Drunkenness, 1914–1935

| | | Arrests for Drunkenness/1,000 | |
| | Cirrhosis Deaths/ | Moderation | World |
Year	100,000	League	League
1914	21.3	18.9	17.5
1915	20.6	18.5	17.3
1916	20.1	19.5	17.8
1917	19.0	18.3	17.0
1918	16.6	13.8	12.9
1919	14.6	9.8	8.8
1920	13.4	7.1	7.0
1921	13.9	9.3	9.6
1922	14.1	12.3	12.9

Rates of Death from Cirrhosis and Arrests for Drunkenness *(continued)*

| | | Arrests for Drunkenness/1,000 | |
Year	*Cirrhosis Deaths/* 100,000	*Moderation* *League*	*World* *League*
1923	13.4		
1924	13.1		
1925	13.1		
1926	12.8		
1927	13.0		
1928	12.8		
1929	12.1		
1930	12.0		
1931	12.1		
1932	11.6		
1933	11.9		
1934	12.0		
1935	12.2		

Sources: For cirrhosis, Jeffrey A. Miron and Jeffrey Zwiebel, "Alcohol Consumption during Prohibition," *American Economic Review* 81, no. 2 (1991): 242–47; for the Moderation League, G. W. Wickersham, *Enforcement of Prohibition Laws,* vol. 5 (Washington, DC: US Government Printing Office, 1931); for the World League, E. H. Cherrington, *The Anti-Saloon League Year Book* (Columbus, OH: The League, 1923), 70–75.

The number of arrests for drunkenness is useful primarily because it provides a distinct measure that can either independently confirm or call into question the trends we see with cirrhosis. Arrests for drunkenness give researchers a view of a wider population of drinkers than does cirrhosis, as any one episode of public drunkenness could result in an arrest, while only habitual heavy drinkers would likely suffer from cirrhosis. Of course, arrests for drunkenness still undercount the total amount of consumption as they do not account for those people who drank only small amounts at any one time and those who drank in the privacy of their own homes, all of whom were less likely to encounter the police than those who drank heavily in public settings.

Further qualifying arrest statistics is the role played by the police themselves, as their discretion determined which interactions with drunkards resulted in arrests. In addition to a host of sociological factors (e.g., class, race, gender) and situational factors (e.g., presence of someone who could take the person home, potential danger to self and others) that might have swayed a police officer's decision, it is possible that the prohibition laws themselves had an impact. Police might have taken drunkenness enforcement more seriously once the law was enacted, resulting in a greater number of arrests. Conversely, if police enforced drunkenness less vigorously (or recorded arrests for drunkenness as prohibition violations rather than as a distinct category), then arrest rates would understate alcohol consumption during prohibition.[7]

The best information available for drunkenness arrests comes from two sources—the World League against Alcoholism, a pro-prohibition organization, and the Moderation League, an anti-prohibition organization. The World League data are based on arrests by 301 urban police departments surveyed between 1910 and 1922; the Moderation League data are based on arrests by 599 urban police departments surveyed between 1914 and 1922. The data for both sets are based on arrests in at least one city in each of forty-seven of the then forty-eight states, and the cities surveyed in each set together accounted for 30–35 percent of the total US population.

Both the World League and the Moderation League found a gradual downward trend in drunkenness arrests beginning prior to federal prohibition, a bottoming out in the year after the passage of the federal amendment, and then a gradual rise. Although the similarities in collection methods and police departments surveyed by each organization would lead us to expect similar arrest rates, the fact that both a pro-prohibition organization and an anti-prohibition one agreed on these basic trends confirms their likely accuracy. These data also match closely the pattern of prohibition's impact on cirrhosis, an initial steep decline followed by a gradual upturn.[8]

Not only did prohibition lower the amount of alcohol Americans drank while the law was in force, but its impact continued to be felt for many years after the law was repealed. Data gathered by the NIAAA put the pre-prohibition high water mark for consumption between the years

1906 and 1910. During that five-year span, the average adult consumption per year ran to 2.6 gallons of pure alcohol, 1.47 gallons of beer, .17 gallons of wine, and .96 gallons of spirits. Americans would not consume that yearly amount of alcohol again until 1973. Pre-prohibition wine consumption would not consistently be exceeded until 1941; spirit consumption, until 1964; and as of 2014 we have yet to reach pre-prohibition levels of beer consumption.[9]

These generational impacts are likely the result of the federal dry law and the many state laws that preceded it, as the cohort born circa 1900 could not drink legally until 1933. By that time, many were likely settled into patterns of abstinence. In addition to the direct impact of the dry laws, there were other, less obvious factors leading to lower consumption. Electoral battles fought over prohibition heightened awareness of the dangers of alcohol. Theater- and moviegoers likely would have seen shows that presented drinkers as flawed characters, while rarely encountering liquor advertisements on billboards, in magazines, or in daily newspapers.[10] Those who visited their doctors probably heard about the American Medical Association's public opposition to both the recreational and therapeutic use of alcohol, as well as newly completed physiological and epidemiological studies claiming that alcohol was a depressant and associating its use with crime, mental illness, and disease.[11] Schoolchildren in every state were required to attend classes on "scientific temperance instruction" as part of their curriculum, and half of the nation's school districts mandated the use of a textbook that portrayed liquor as invariably addictive poison.[12] Such an emphasis on the evils associated with drink would likely have convinced many that even if it was legal, alcohol was a substance best used in moderation or perhaps not at all. Taken together, then, all the available evidence we have makes clear that the statement "prohibition increased alcohol consumption" is indeed a myth. Fewer people drank during the prohibition era and for several decades afterwards.

Before we concede unequivocal victory for the prohibitionists, a few caveats are in order. First, while alcohol consumption clearly fell during prohibition and after, consumption levels were still nowhere close to zero, putting the lie to dry campaigners' promises of a sober society. Further weakening the prohibitionist case were the costs the law brought with it, among them decreases in tax revenue, increases in gang violence, corruption, and deaths due to consumption of bad liquor.[13] Much of this is easily seen in hindsight. No law is 100 percent effective, and in suggesting otherwise for federal prohibition drys were raising public expectations too high.

If prohibitionists can justly be accused of overselling the hoped-for outcomes of a dry law, the anti-prohibitionists can be chastised for underselling its actual effects. The myth that prohibition didn't work and everybody was drinking comes largely from wet campaigners seeking repeal.[14] Like the drys, the wets were not wholly wrong. Alcohol consumption rates were rising as the repeal movement hit its peak in the early 1930s, and it is likely that wet campaigners traveled in social circles in which many folks drank. But "some" or "many" drinkers was not an actual increase in consumption; to suggest otherwise unnecessarily muddies the waters, making it harder to craft policies rooted in our collective experience.

What I think this points to is an admonition to be wary of claims-makers and their simple panaceas offered to combat complex social problems. Participants in social movements have a vested interest in their own point of view. Not only are they the most likely to be "true believers," but they are also likely to have spent the most time and energy in pursuit of their cause and to have had their lives shaped by that cause. It's understandable that decades of mostly fruitless campaigning against the saloon (see earlier essays in this volume) could bring dry activists to the point of just wanting to get rid of all the saloons; it is equally understandable that frustration with an unenforceable law led many wets to argue for repeal. But just because activists are frustrated doesn't mean they are right. Those of us who are less emotionally involved need to take the measure of such claims and push policymakers to enact legislation that will address conditions as they are, not as they appear to be.

NOTES

1. For more on Mayor Walker and especially his attitudes toward prohibition, see Michael Lerner, *Dry Manhattan: Prohibition in New York City* (Cambridge, MA: Harvard University Press, 2007).

2. In addition to several essays in this volume, among the many fine works on prohibition and enforcement are W. J. Rorabaugh, *The Alcoholic Republic: An American Tradition* (New York: Oxford University Press, 1979); Lerner, *Dry Manhattan;* and Lisa McGirr, *The War on Alcohol: Prohibition and the Rise of the American State* (New York: Norton, 2016).

3. Economic analyses of prohibition, largely negative, are almost as old as the law itself. See, e.g., Irving Fisher, *Prohibition at its Worst* (New York: Alcohol Information Committee, 1927); and Clark Warburton, *The Economic Results of Prohibition* (New York: Columbia University Press, 1932). For a more recent economic analysis, see Mark Thornton, *The Economics of Prohibition* (Salt Lake City: University of Utah Press, 1991).

4. See, e.g., Robert E. Mann, Lise Anglin, Karl Wilkins, Evelyn R. Vingilis, and Scott Macdonald, "Mortality in a Sample of Convicted Drinking Drivers," *Addiction* 88 (1993): 643–47; and M. J. Thun R. Peto, A. D. Lopez, J. H. Monaco, S. J. Henley, C. W. Heath Jr., and R. Doll, "Alcohol Consumption and Mortality among Middle-Aged and Elderly U.S. Adults," *New England Journal of Medicine* 337 (1997): 1705–14.

5. The best sources here are Merton M. Hyman, *Drinkers, Drinking, and Alcohol-Related Mortality and Hospitalizations: A Statistical Compendium* (New Brunswick, NJ: Rutgers University Press, 1980); and Young-Hee Yoon and Chiung M. Chen, *Liver Cirrhosis Mortality in the United States, 1970–98,* Surveillance Report 57 (Washington, DC: US Department of Health and Human Services, National Institute on Alcohol Abuse and Alcoholism, 2001).

6. Among the research confirming these results are Paul Aaron and David Musto, "Temperance and Prohibition in America: A Historical Overview," in *Alcohol and Public Policy: Beyond the Shadow of Prohibition,* ed. Mark H. Moore and Dean R Gerstein (Washington, DC: National Academies Press, 1981), 127–81; Griffith Edwards, Peter Anderson, Thomas F. Babor, Sally Casswell, Roberta Ferrence, Norman Giesbrecht, Christine Godfrey, Harold D. Holder, and Paul H. M. M. Lemmens, *Alcohol Policy and the Public Good* (New York: Oxford University Press, 1994); Yoon and Chen, *Liver Cirrhosis Mortality in the United States,* 27.

7. The best discussion of policing in the United States historically is Eric Monkonnen, *Police in Urban America, 1860–1920* (London: Cambridge University Press, 1981).

8. Other research examining the relationship of prohibition using arrests for drunkenness includes Angela Dills, Mireille Jacobson, and Jeffrey A. Miron, "The Effect of Alcohol Prohibition on Alcohol Consumption: Evidence from Drunkenness Arrests," *Economics Letters* 86 (2005): 279–84; and Jeffrey A. Miron and Jeffrey Zwiebel, "Alcohol Consumption during Prohibition," *American Economic Review* 81, no. 2 (1991): 242–47.

9. Sarah P. Haughwout and Megan E. Slater, *Apparent Per Capita Alcohol Consumption: National, State and Regional Trends, 1977–2016,* Surveillance Report 110 (Washington,

DC: US Department of Health and Human Services, National Institute on Alcohol Abuse and Alcoholism, 2018), 12.

10. Joan Silverman, "I'll Never Touch Another Drop: Images of Alcohol and Temperance in American Popular Culture, 1874–1919" (PhD diss., New York University, 1979); Silverman, "The Birth of a Nation: Prohibition Propaganda," *Southern Quarterly* 19 (1981): 23–30.

11. James Timberlake, *Prohibition and the Progressive Movement, 1900–1920* (Cambridge, MA: Harvard University Press, 1963); Denise Herd, "Ideology, History and Changing Models of Liver Cirrhosis Epidemiology," *British Journal of Addiction* 87 (1992): 1113–26; Brian Katcher, "The Post-Repeal Eclipse in Knowledge about the Harmful Effects of Alcohol," *Addiction* 88 (June 1993): 729–44.

12. Jonathan Zimmerman, *Distilling Democracy: Alcohol Education in America's Public Schools, 1880–1925* (Lawrence: University Press of Kansas, 1999).

13. Some of these negative outcomes are taken up more fully in later essays in this volume. Scholars have suggested that a reason not to drink might have been bad booze, which would have achieved the prohibitionist intent through more convoluted means.

14. Thomas Pegram's essay in this volume discusses the repeal movement in greater detail. Among the best scholarly sources on repeal are Rorabaugh, *Alcoholic Republic;* and David E. Kyvig, *Repealing National Prohibition,* 2nd ed. (Kent, OH: Kent State University Press, 2000).

MYTH 6

PROHIBITION STARTED ORGANIZED CRIME

RICHARD F. HAMM

A century after prohibition's adoption, the myth persists that it started organized crime. For instance, when I began a Google search with the phrase "How did prohibition . . . ," not far down the list of suggested search phrases was "how did prohibition lead to organized crime?" Clearly, a good number of the searching public make the implicit assumption that prohibition spawned organized crime. Their unstated premise is that before national prohibition there was no, or little, organized crime. The lavish and lurid way that the press covered bootlegging criminal enterprises of the 1920s made it seem that way at the time, and several generations of history popularizers have kept the myth alive. Yet scholars long ago proved that there was organized crime before prohibition and that the national policy only provided unparalleled opportunity for expansion and development of such crime. When it came to crime, prohibition did much more. Prohibition expanded tremendously the capacity and reach of the federal police, it revolutionized how the federal government prosecuted crime, it put the nation on the path to building the carceral state, and it stimulated the development of American constitutional-law doctrines.

UNORGANIZED AND ORGANIZED CRIME

Across the country, cities held New Year's Eve–like celebrations to mark the coming of national prohibition at midnight on January 17, 1920. They consumed soon-to-be-illegal alcoholic beverages. In New York City, they continued to do so after midnight with no legal consequences. As the historian W. J. Rorabaugh wryly notes, "How long did prohibition last in New York? About two minutes." People drank throughout the era, prompting others to break the law to manufacture, transport (including import), and sell the alcohol. As the ban prompted a rise in prices, many people stepped into the business of bootlegging. Some were just continuing what they had already been doing in dry territory before prohibition, but for others it was a new venture. For instance, according to my maternal grandmother, during prohibition her mother ran a saloon "for the men" out of her kitchen in the Bronx. For her Italian and Italian American customers she supplied home-produced wine. To protect her business, she paid off the police and informed on others who set up similar shops. Her example was also typical. Most prohibition violation was small-scale crime. In Virginia, during the years of its prohibition (1916–33) state (not federal) officers seized around thirty thousand stills. The high number underscores the small scale of the production of illegal alcohol there. Yet, an illegal business was still a business, and some used modern business methods (and much more) to garner huge profits. Those who did so became the organized-crime syndicates upon which the myth expands.[1]

Before national prohibition, there was an established, city-centered business of crime. There were strong connections between purveyors of vice (such as gambling and prostitution) and corrupt officials, who allowed gambling, prostitution, and drinking to take place regardless of bans on such activities. While thriving, this crime business was small scale. How blatant the vice varied from city to city and from time to time. When the vice businesses were particularly above board and the corruption of government an open secret, a city was said to be "wide open." In the opposite case, the "lid was shut down." Liquor prohibition opened up a new field to existing (and new) criminals, as the market for liquor did not vanish with the disappearance of legal liquor, even though consumption declined during prohibition. The lucrative nature of the illegal liquor trade prompted the expansion of organized crime. The gangs took into their own hands the production, the transportation, and the supplying of retailers. They built sophisticated and elaborate networks to carry on their illegal enterprises. Gangs flourished in most American communities of any size. By the end of the era, they were large, varied, and no longer just local. Some, like Chicago's crime syndicate (first headed by Johnny Torrio and then by Al Capone), were shockingly brazen and violent. Whether violent or not, these gangs contributed significantly to the corruption of local government and law enforcement at all levels. While the mass media—including newspapers, periodicals, and film—chronicled these criminals' corruption, they also romanticized them, virtually making them into folk heroes. By supplying the rich and the poor and catering to the respectable who drank in their homes as well as the disreputable who drank in dives, these criminals made organized crime a part of American life. With the repeal of prohibition, organized crime survived; it returned to its older businesses, including prostitution and gambling, and embraced new endeavors, such as illegal drugs and labor rackets.[2]

FEDERAL POLICE

The place of prohibition in the creation of the federal police has been aptly described by Lawrence Friedman, a leading authority on US legal history: "Probably nothing in the first half of the twentieth century matched prohibition in expanding the federal [anti]crime effort." Before national prohibition, there was not much of a federal police force. There were Secret Service officers, Federal Bureau of Investigation agents, and Post Office inspectors. Their roles were usually defined by the scope of federal-government powers; thus the Secret Service protected the currency, while the postal inspectors guarded mostly against mail fraud.

The FBI's vague and shifting mission expanded with the growth of government. For example, while not designated the chief enforcer of the Mann Act, the FBI took it upon itself to enforce the act and opened field offices in various cities to do so. Thus, the federal government patched together a national police, with agents in various departments. Yet, its policing capacity was quite limited and it did not reach the great mass of Americans.[3]

The creators of the Eighteenth Amendment had not envisioned that their work would create a huge expansion of federal authority or require tremendous growth in federal law enforcement. Most American states were dry at the time of the adoption of the amendment, leading prohibition advocates to believe that prohibition was already well entrenched. Moreover, the amendment declared that the federal government and states would have concurrent power to enforce the policy. The leading dry organization, the Anti-Saloon League, thought hiring a great number of new federal officers would be unnecessary because the larger number of state officials would do a better job for less money. But they would do so under the direction of the federal government's law, which would set the policy, the most important being that an alcoholic beverage was one containing .5 percent or more alcohol.

The 1920 Volstead Act, which provided for the enforcement of the Eighteenth Amendment, and the federal enforcement system rested on these ideas. Drawing on years of state experience with prohibition, the Volstead Act created a great number of ways for the federal government to enforce prohibition. The penalties ranged from fines to condemnation of buildings or vehicles used in the illegal trade as nuisances to prison time. These provisions mirrored those in existence in already dry states. In addition, prohibition was to be enforced by existing federal officers, such as Customs Office officials, Coast Guard agents, and Post Office inspectors. Yet, the Volstead Act also created new federal police: prohibition agents. Because of the federal government's long history of regulating liquor through taxation, the new force was placed in the Treasury Department. Drys hoped to be able to influence these officers, so the act exempted the prohibition agents from the civil-service laws, which would have required the applicants for the jobs to pass certain minimum standards and would have reduced the efforts of politicians to put their friends and supporters in office. In addition, their number was kept low; initially there were only fifteen hundred officers.[4]

However, the responsibilities of the federal officers expanded, as the states did not do their share of the enforcement work. The idea that the federal government had a role in law enforcement proved an excellent pretense for states to give up their responsibilities for prohibition enforcement. State legislatures, as a whole, refused to allocate much money for the implementation of prohibition because they said the national government should pay. Some states' officials did as little as they could, routinely referring questions about prohibition enforcement to the local federal prohibition agent. The reasons for state giving up on prohibition varied. In some states it was unpopular, while in other states reducing government spending was key. Whatever the cause, the federal government ended up taking the lead in prohibition enforcement.[5]

The prohibition federal agents were not up to the task of curtailing the massive violation of the prohibition law. When state and local efforts faltered, Congress refused to significantly expand their numbers. By 1929 there were only 1,886 agents. Moreover, the civil-service exemption resulted in the appointment of men who were owed favors by leading politicians. Obviously, some of these officers entered these positions for the potential to earn money (legally and illegally) rather than because they were interested in doing the job. In a six-year period beginning in 1920, 752 prohibition officials lost their jobs for delinquency or misconduct, with drunkenness and bribery being the two main reasons for dismissal. Late reforms extending civil-service rules to prohibition agents in 1927 and placing officers in the Department of Justice in 1930 were too little too late.

While unequal to the task of fully implementing the alcohol ban, the prohibition-enforcement machinery considerably expanded the federal police presence in American life. In 1930 the complement of 1,450 frontline prohibition agents dwarfed the 350 FBI field agents. They were the largest federal law-enforcement body. Furthermore, prohibition agents engaged in activities that directly affected people. In the nine years from 1921 to 1929 they made 539,759 arrests, an average of 59,973 arrests per year. In the same period, prohibition agents seized 45,177 cars in the course of their duties. By their own account, the prohibition bureau agents killed 89 people, though later repeal advocates claimed that they had killed thousands. While the trigger-happiness of the federal agents drew headlines, their mundane arrests for violation of prohibition challenged federal prosecutors.[6]

FEDERAL PROSECUTORS

The period of national prohibition transformed how the federal government prosecuted crime. At the beginning of national prohibition, there was virtually no coordination between investigators of crime and prosecutors. US attorneys, attached to each federal district court jurisdiction, were patronage appointees under the loose authority of the Justice Department. They took the cases that other federal officials developed for them and exercised great latitude in deciding whether to prosecute fully or not. Beginning in 1921 and ending in 1929, Assistant Attorney General Mabel Walker Willebrandt led the Justice Department's campaign to enforce prohibition, reorienting how the federal government prosecuted crime. Later twentieth-century prosecutions against organized crime and drug smuggling rings owe their nature to the innovations of the prohibition era.

The Justice Department developed policies for the US attorneys to follow. For example, it encouraged US attorneys to bring conspiracy charges instead of charges for merely violating the liquor law and provided support for those attorneys who did so. To follow through, Willebrandt instigated a special squad of prosecutors to act when federal attorneys proved inept or corrupt. Similarly, in 1924, under the direction of Attorney General Harlan Fiske Stone, she compiled a statistical analysis of the prohibition prosecutions of each of the US attorneys' offices. Stone used this information to pressure attorneys to prosecute more cases or to arrange for their resignations. Though limited by the intricacies of political patronage, which dominated appointments, Willebrandt's actions represented a significant attempt to systemize the prosecution of crime. A mark of her success in bureaucratic terms can be seen in the growth of her staff, from three assistants in 1921 to more than a hundred in 1929.[7]

The expansion was necessary because prohibition led to a significant expansion of federal-court activity. In the thirteen full fiscal years of national prohibition (1921–33), cases arising from the violation of the federal prohibition-enforcement laws in the district court dockets averaged 64.6 percent of all federal cases. Equally telling are the raw numbers. In 1921, there were 29,114 prohibition cases, while in 1932 there were 65,960. At the same time, the overall number of cases handled by the federal district courts increased significantly. In 1921 there were 54,487 federal criminal cases; in 1932 the total reached 92,174. It was not just the numbers but also the impact of the publicity of the trials that brought federal-court actions to the attention of the American public. Willebrandt and her staff used their prosecutions especially to generate headlines. A number of times, Willebrandt supervised a prosecution or sat in the courtroom while one of her assistants pressed the case. Since women government lawyers were quite a novelty in the 1920s, her actions generated press coverage. Similarly, she focused on headline-grabbing corruption cases in both the federal and local governments. This seeking of press notice was not gratuitous; it was part of a Justice Department campaign to showcase prohibition-enforcement activity and make a case for cleaner government to the public. At the same time, it was designed to involve regular people and organizations in the war against liquor. While the public-relations efforts dominated the news coverage, routine prosecutions continued. Thanks to high rates of plea bargains (an innovation for federal courts of this era) and dropped charges, the percentage of convictions in prohibition cases from 1922 to 1933 averaged above 82 percent.[8]

Prohibition also contributed to the increase in federal-prison populations and prompted changes in prison administration that made the carceral state possible. In the era of national prohibition, the number of federal prisoners grew dramatically. In 1923 there were 4,664 federal prisoners, while seven years later there were 12,964. In 1923, 5 percent of all US inmates were in federal custody, compared with more than 10 percent in 1930. The growth rate in state and federal prison populations duplicated this pattern. During the middle of the period of national prohibition (1923–30) the number of federal prisoners increased by a factor of 2.77. In the same period, the population in state prisons increased by a factor of 1.39. The population in federal prisons was growing twice as fast as the population in state prisons.[9]

Many of these new federal prisoners, but never a majority, were incarcerated for violating prohibition. The rate of imprisonment for prohibition violation, based on new commitments to federal prisons, showed upward growth through the era. For the period 1919–24 the rate was 6.9 percent; for 1924–29, 17.1 percent; and for 1929–34, 43.4 percent. The penalties of the Volstead Act in part explain the relatively low number imprisoned for violation of federal liquor laws. The Volstead Act's most common mode of punishment was a fine. Thus, the increasing of federal penalties in 1929 explains the sharp spurt at the end of prohibition. Indeed, in 1930, the first year the new law was in force, almost half of all new federal prisoners—49 percent—had violated federal liquor laws. This influx of new prisoners taxed the existing system of federal prisons and prompted its expansion and reorganization. At the opening of national prohibition, there were only three federal prisons for men. Generally, space in these prisons was reserved for those serving long sentences; short-term male prisoners and female prisoners were boarded in various state facilities. Prisons, staffed through a patronage process, were rife with corruption and mismanagement. For the most part, federal institutions did not follow the practices prescribed by penology professionals, such as segregation of young, impressionable offenders from older, seasoned prisoners and establishment of prison industries to facilitate rehabilitation. During prohibition, the federal government expanded the number of its prisons to fourteen, adding women's and young offenders' institutions as well as institutions to hold people before trial. Moreover, in 1930 Congress created the Bureau of Prisons in the Justice Department. It put penal professionals in charge of the system and began instituting many of the practices used widely in the states. Thus prohibition helped build the tools and infrastructure used during later criminal scares and crackdowns.[10]

NEW CONSTITUTIONAL LAW

All the federal criminal trials coming from the tremendous expansion of federal policing prompted the courts to expand significantly American constitutional law. During national prohibition, federal courts laid the foundation for a significant body of new constitutional law limiting police action and regulating the conduct of federal law-enforcement officials. In the years from 1920 to 1933, federal appeals courts reshaped the law of entrapment, search and seizure, double jeopardy, property forfeiture, and trial by jury. Moreover, the development of these constitutional doctrines followed a pattern. The courts, especially the Supreme Court, first supported enforcement actions over individual rights, then drifted into ambivalence toward the policy, and at the end of the prohibition era asserted people's rights against government actions.[11]

The prohibition era's search-and-seizure cases exemplify the range and nature of these important doctrinal developments. Before the adoption of the Eighteenth Amendment, the Supreme Court had created an exclusionary rule banning the use of evidence seized in violation of the Fourth Amendment. Moreover, it had declared that the Fourth Amendment was to be liberally construed to protect the rights of the people. The policy of national prohibition tremendously expanded the number of search-and-seizures issues, generating more than five hundred federal appellate cases. The ones that reached the Supreme Court resulted in a narrowing of the reach of the Fourth Amendment.

In 1924 the Supreme Court ruled that the Fourth Amendment was not violated when government agents saw evidence of lawbreaking in plain sight, such as outside a house, and thus they did not need a warrant to make a search. In the 1925 case of *Carroll v. United States,* the Court refused to overturn the convictions of bootleggers whose car had been stopped and searched by federal prohibition agents without a warrant. The Court determined that since the agents had had good reason to suspect that the car was engaged in illegal activity, and since the car could have fled before a warrant was obtained, the search was not a violation of the Fourth Amendment's prohibition of unreasonable searches. Similarly, in *Olmstead v. United States* the Court ruled, over notable dissents by Louis Brandeis and Oliver Wendell Holmes Jr., that since federal agents who had tapped the phone lines leading to homes and offices of notorious bootleggers had not entered the premises, they had not conducted a search. Thus, evidence gathered by wiretapping was not an unreasonable search under the Fourth Amendment and did not compel the defendants to be witnesses against themselves, contrary to the Fifth Amendment.[12]

As individual and systematic excesses in enforcement emerged, a reaction set in that limited government searches. Some justices, most notably Louis Brandeis, began to worry about protecting people from government agents. By the early 1930s the Supreme Court had rediscovered its liberal pre-prohibition Fourth Amendment rulings. Limiting the holdings in previous cases to certain circumstances and creating new exceptions, the Court applied these ideals to new prohibition cases, reducing the effect of previous prohibition rulings. In 1932, in *Taylor v. United States,* the Court held that a garage at the edge of a defendant's property fell under the Volstead Act's stipulation that searches of domiciles be carried out under a warrant. In turn, Congress essentially outlawed law-enforcement wiretapping in the 1934 Communications Act and prohibited the use of evidence gathered by such methods in federal court. Indeed, by the end of the prohibition era the Court and Congress were balancing the privacy of individuals with the needs of law enforcement, thus laying the foundation for modern search-and-seizure doctrines. These liberal doctrines, which emerged at the end of the period, would be the precedents later relied on by the Warren Court when it applied the Fourth Amendment's restrictions to the states.[13]

At the same time that they remade constitutional law, federal jurists took on the role of overseer of federal police. Judges, through the case law, exercised a supervisory role over the prohibition agency and its agents. This development occurred in part because court rulings constrained the actions of the federal police and in part as a result of the general notion that the government itself could become a lawbreaker through the actions of its officers. Judges distinguished between ends and means, arguing that the legitimate ends of prohibition could not be reached by illegitimate means. In a number of opinions, judges criticized what they perceived as agent misconduct, be it invasions of the home, activities that could entice people into committing crime, or the too free use of their weapons. If federal agents displayed lawlessness, the courts would refuse to sanction their activities. For example, in a 1931 case the Supreme Court refused to allow a conviction to stand because federal agents had lied about having a warrant. These supervisory statements and rulings by federal judges presaged much of the mid-twentieth-century's jurisprudence of due process and rights.[14]

CONCLUSION

Beyond stimulating the tremendous expansion of organized crime, national prohibition prompted an expansion of the federal police. An expanded role for federal police became both a governmental norm and a reality in people's lives. This new norm did not disappear with the end of prohibition. Indeed, with repeal came expanded federal taxation of liquor, which required almost the same level of enforcement and regulation by the national government. More importantly, the nation had gotten used to expanded federal police activity. And, during the Depression—in response to the perception that gangsterism, kidnappings, and bank robberies were on the rise—Congress created a host of new federal policing responsibilities. Attorney General Homer Cummings, following the path pioneered by Willebrandt, orchestrated a campaign of enforcement, prosecution, and publicity designed to create a grass-roots movement against crime. The chief beneficiary of this campaign was the Federal Bureau of Investigation. The FBI, under J. Edgar Hoover, hitched the publicity wave of the war against crime to scientific and professional policing and emerged as the federal government's main policing agency. The people it arrested were prosecuted by a more professional Justice Department staff and, if convicted (provided that the government did not violate their due process rights in arresting or trying them), incarcerated in one of the growing number of federal prisons. Thus prohibition helped construct part of the modern American state.

NOTES

1. W. J. Rorabaugh, *Prohibition: A Concise History* (New York: Oxford University Press, 2018), 60; Lisa McGirr, *The War on Alcohol: Prohibition and the Rise of the American State* (New York: Norton, 2016), 78.

2. Eric A. Monkhonen, ed., *Crime and Justice in American History: Historical Articles on the Origins and Evolution of American Criminal Justice,* vol. 8 (Munich: K. G. Sauer, 1992), pts. 1 and 2; Mark H. Haller, *Illegal Enterprise: the Work of Historian Mark Haller,* ed. Matthew G. Yeager (Lanham, MD: University Press of American, 2013); Daniel Okrent, *Last Call: The Rise and Fall of Prohibition* (New York: Scribner, 2010), 272–77; Humbert S. Nelli, "American Syndicate Crime: A Legacy of Prohibition," in *Law, Alcohol, and Order: Perspectives on National Prohibition,* ed. David E. Kyvig (Westport, CT: Greenwood, 1985), 123–37; Mark H. Haller, "Bootleggers as Businessmen: From City Slums to City Builders," in Kyvig, *Law, Alcohol, and Order,* 139–57; Kristofer Allerfeldt, *Crime and the Rise of Modern America: A History from 1865–1941* (New York: Routledge, 2011), 135–36.

3. Lawrence M. Friedman, *Crime and Punishment in American History* (New York: Basic Books, 1993), 261–74, quotation at 265; David R. Johnson, *American Law Enforcement: A History* (St. Louis: Forum, 1981), 73–87, 167–76; David J. Langum, *Crossing over the Line: Legislating Morality and the Mann Act* (Chicago: University of Chicago Press, 1994), 49. McGirr, *War on Alcohol,* 208–10, discusses the rise of the Border Patrol thanks to prohibition.

4. Richard F. Hamm, *Shaping the Eighteenth Amendment: Temperance Reform, Legal Culture, and Polity* (Chapel Hill: University of North Carolina Press, 1995), 242–55.

5. Rorabaugh, *Prohibition,* 72–73.

6. Richard F. Hamm. "Short Euphorias Followed by Long Hangovers: Unintended Consequences of the Eighteenth and Twenty-first Amendments," in *Unintended Consequences of Constitutional Amendment,* ed. David E. Kyvig (Athens: University of Georgia Press, 2000), 177–78; Rayman L. Solomon, "Regulating the Regulators: Prohibition Enforcement in the Seventh Circuit," in Kyvig, *Law, Alcohol, and Order,* 93; McGirr, *War on Alcohol,* 209.

7. Dorothy M. Brown, *Mabel Walker Willebrandt: A Study of Power, Loyalty, and Law* (Knoxville: University of Tennessee Press, 1984), 49–80.

8. Hamm, "Short Euphorias," 179–80.

9. Hamm, "Short Euphorias," 179–80.

10. Hamm, "Short Euphorias," 179–80; McGirr, *War on Alcohol,* 203.

11. Kenneth M. Murchison, *Federal Criminal Law Doctrines: The Forgotten Influence of National Prohibition* (Durham, NC: Duke University Press, 1994), 74–103; Okrent, *Last Call,* 283–84; John J. Guthrie Jr., *Keepers of the Spirits: The Judicial Response to Prohibition Enforcement in Florida, 1885–1935* (Westport, CT: Greenwood, 1998).

12. *Hester v. United States,* 265 U.S. 57; *Carroll v. United States,* 267 U.S. 132; *Olmstead v. United States,* 277 U.S. 438; Richard F. Hamm, "*Olmstead v. United States:* The Constitutional Challenges of Prohibition Enforcement," a unit on *Olmstead v. United States* for the Teaching the History of the Federal Courts project of the Federal Judicial Center, http://www.fjc.gov/history/home.nsf/page/tu_olmstead_background.html.

13. *Taylor v. United States,* 286 U.S. 1; Wesley M. Oliver, *The Prohibition Era and Policing: A Legacy of Misregulation* (Nashville, TN: Vanderbilt University Press, 2018).

14. *Go-Bart Importing Co. v. United States,* 282 U.S. 344; Solomon, "Regulating the Regulators," 81–96.

MYTH 7

REPEAL HAPPENED BECAUSE PROHIBITION WAS A FAILURE

THOMAS R. PEGRAM

It is a convenient myth that fundamental flaws in the adoption and enforcement of national constitutional prohibition compelled the American people to repeal the Eighteenth Amendment and sensibly abandon the misguided effort to regulate the personal behavior of American drinkers. Honest observers, including many drys, noted the crippling shortcomings of prohibition enforcement, but few believed that repeal of the Eighteenth Amendment was possible. Moreover, despite its detractors, prohibition compiled some achievements and retained resourceful defenders during the dry 1920s. On the average, Americans drank less because of prohibition. Historians estimate that alcohol consumption among Americans fifteen years of age and older dropped by half during national prohibition and did not surpass pre-prohibition levels until 1970. National prohibition also eliminated the brewery-owned "old-time" saloon that had shaped American drinking culture prior to the 1920s. My great-grandfather William Dickmeyer managed a brewery-owned saloon in Fort Wayne, Indiana, until the onset of prohibition. When he died in 1922, his occupation was listed as "Prop[rietor]

soft drink parlor." Even the major anti-prohibition organizations joined
in the condemnation of saloons. Deeply unpopular in the Northeast, in
cities, and in ethnic and working-class communities across the nation,
prohibition nevertheless remained a reform aspiration for many Americans and seemed safely locked into the Constitution.[1]

The success of the repeal movement grew out of the shattering impact of the Great Depression and the careful cultivation of public sentiment by well-organized interest groups. Economic collapse demolished
the purported connection between dry reforms and prosperity and focused dissatisfaction on Herbert Hoover's administration. As the 1929
crash deepened into depression, Hoover and the Republican Party became proponents of invigorated prohibition enforcement. Conservative
business leaders in the Association Against the Prohibition Amendment
(AAPA) joined the Women's Organization for National Prohibition Reform (WONPR) to rehabilitate the image of wet resistance from that of
self-interested drinkers and the liquor industry to respectable defenders of American institutions. Assisted by legal experts, anti-prohibition
associations directed public sentiment into pressure for political action
to pass a repeal amendment. Ratification of the Twenty-First Amendment turned on the little-used constitutional mechanism of elected state
conventions, thus bypassing the political influence of dry lobbyists over
state legislators and drawing on the surging popular opinion in favor of
ending prohibition.

THE STATUS OF CONSTITUTIONAL PROHIBITION

The failure of national prohibition as a policy was reinforced by the
repeal of the Eighteenth Amendment in 1933, the only constitutional
amendment ever to be so effaced. Complaints about prohibition had accumulated over the 1920s. Some resented the intrusiveness of the dry
reform into private life and local governance. Many Americans decried
its inconsistent, often inept, and sometimes brutal enforcement. Critics also highlighted the widespread evasion of the Volstead Act and its

state-level counterparts and worried about the disregard for law and authority that such defiance produced. Beginning with New York in 1923, several states repealed their state enforcement statutes and called for modification of national dry standards. The National Commission on Law Observance and Enforcement, known as the Wickersham Commission and authorized by the Hoover administration to examine national prohibition, confirmed prohibition's shortcomings in its 1931 report. "It is evident," the commission concluded, "that, taking the country as a whole, people of wealth, business men and professional men, and their families, and, perhaps, the higher paid workingmen and their families, are drinking in large numbers in quite frank disregard of the declared policy of the National Prohibition Act."[2]

Opponents and supporters of prohibition alike, however, acknowledged that weaknesses in the prohibition regime did not clear a path for repeal of the Eighteenth Amendment. Until at least 1928, most informed observers agreed that it would be impossible to remove the Eighteenth Amendment from the Constitution. William Howard Taft, who opposed the adoption of national prohibition but then, as chief justice of the Supreme Court, rigorously supported its enforcement, stated, "There isn't the slightest chance that the constitutional amendment will be repealed. You know that and I know it." Clarence Darrow, a fervent wet, regretfully agreed with Taft. "The fact is that Prohibition is entrenched today in the fundamental law of the nation," he sadly concluded in 1924. "Even to modify the Volstead Act would require a political revolution; to repeal the Eighteenth Amendment is well-nigh inconceivable." The Yale economist Irving Fisher, a prominent defender of prohibition, cheerfully reiterated Darrow's admission that the dry voters of thirteen states could block repeal. Thirty-five states had implemented statewide prohibition at the time the Eighteenth Amendment was ratified. Even though prohibition had suffered setbacks, Fisher confidently stated in 1926 that "no one pretends that [prohibition support] has lost enough to have the slightest chance of repealing the Eighteenth Amendment." Asserting that modification of the Volstead Act required the "impossible" step of repealing the Eighteenth Amendment, Fisher concluded that "the only honorable course left" was to shore up the weaknesses in national prohibition and "enforce the law."[3]

The US government and the Hoover administration followed Fisher's admonition. In the latter 1920s, government administrative reformers acted to correct structural inefficiencies, improve professionalism among field agents, and centralize control over the mechanism of national prohibition. Civil-service advocates and structural reformers championed the reorganization act of 1927, which removed prohibition enforcement from the Internal Revenue Service and instead created the Bureau of Prohibition, headed by a commissioner of prohibition under the appointive authority of the secretary of the treasury. Federal prohibition employees and agents came under civil-service rules, thus undercutting the political arrangements by which Wayne Wheeler, of the Anti-Saloon League, controlled the selection of agents and reducing the widespread corruption and incompetence that had dogged federal prohibition enforcement. In 1930, a second piece of legislation, recommended by the Wickersham Commission in its preliminary report and endorsed by President Herbert Hoover, transferred the Prohibition Bureau from Treasury to the Department of Justice.[4]

Under Hoover, further commitments to enforcing prohibition by means of centralized government authority were embodied in the harsh provisions of the Jones "five and ten" law, which drastically increased prison sentences and fines for prohibition violators, and the president's initiative to build additional federal prisons to house offenders. Driven by prohibition arrests and convictions, the entire criminal justice system expanded. Prison populations in the United States tripled during the life span of national prohibition. Among long-term offenders in federal prisons in 1930, those convicted for violating the Volstead Act made up the largest single group. Rather than accepting the unworkability of national prohibition, Hoover appeared determined to enforce the Eighteenth Amendment. Acknowledgment of these renewed efforts to bolster enforcement led to a much-noticed inconsistency in the conclusions of the Wickersham Commission report in 1931. Although an overwhelming majority of the eleven commissioners in their individual statements emphasized the failures of national prohibition and endorsed amendment or repeal, the report noted "the vigorous and better organized efforts which have gone on since the Bureau of Prohibition Act, 1927" and suggested additional improvements to enforcement. One faction of commissioners was "not convinced that Prohibition under the Eighteenth Amendment is unenforceable and believe[d] that a further trial should be made" before attempting revision of the Eighteenth Amendment. The second group believed that revision of the Eighteenth Amendment was necessary but recommended "improvement of the enforcement agencies" during the time it would take to produce, pass, and ratify a new amendment. Despite its many ailments, national prohibition did not appear likely to vanish overnight.[5]

FROM NULLIFICATION TO REPEAL

Wet resistance to the legal status of national prohibition floundered for most of the 1920s. Early attempts to challenge the constitutionality of the Eighteenth Amendment were swiftly rejected by the Supreme Court. Congress remained dry and unmoved by wet appeals throughout the 1920s. Until he died in 1927 from a heart attack, the Anti-Saloon League's national legislative superintendent, Wayne Wheeler, kept Congress in a headlock. For instance, the terrier-like Wheeler boasted that the 1924 elections had produced a Senate with a 72–24 prohibition majority and a reliably dry House comprising 319 prohibition supporters and only 105 wets. A quartet of senators derisively nicknamed the BEER Group by Wheeler (Maryland's William Cabell Bruce, Edward I. Edwards and Walter E. Edge of New Jersey, and Missourian James Reed) denounced prohibition in public hearings, but they could not alter the Eighteenth Amendment. Even after Wheeler's death, the political parties remained circumspect. Both Republican and Democratic party platforms in 1928 quietly backed enforcement of prohibition laws, even though the Democratic nominee Al Smith declared his personal support for legal beer and advocated returning alcohol regulation to state and local jurisdictions.[6]

Blocked by the courts, Congress, and political parties and despairing of the possibility of repealing the Eighteenth Amendment, opponents of prohibition turned to the strategy of nullification, that is, refusal to enforce an unpopular or misguided law. In some cities and wet enclaves—Baltimore, San Francisco, New Orleans, and Detroit the most prominent among them—the Volstead Act was mostly ignored by local authorities, although federal agents continued to make arrests. Maryland refused to pass a state enforcement law. Local officials determined enforcement in California. In San Francisco County, the Board of Supervisors officially opposed requiring peace officers to enforce prohibition, the county sheriff was a wet politician, and the district attorney also was the state vice president of the AAPA. New York took a step toward more formal nullification when it repealed its enforcement law in 1923. Sympathetic scholars and journalists attempted to build a case for the legitimacy of nullification. The former Yale University president Arthur Twining Hadley argued that northern communities had nullified the despised Fugitive Slave Law in the 1850s. Disobedience of national prohibition laws, he suggested, might carry the same moral weight. "Nullification . . . is not revolution," Hadley claimed. "It is the safety valve which helps a self-governing community avoid the alternative between tyranny and revolution." The journalist Walter Lippmann also endorsed "orderly disobedience . . . which is open, frankly avowed, and in conformity with the general sense of what is reasonable."[7]

Drys harshly criticized the nullification argument. Wheeler denounced repeal of New York's prohibition-enforcement statute as "a direct encouragement to lawlessness." Numerous prohibition supporters emphasized the duty of citizens to obey the Constitution. "The Eighteenth Amendment is part of our fundamental law," declared Pennsylvania governor Gifford Pinchot, "and anyone who breaks it breaks the fundamental law, is a law-breaker, and should be treated as such." Idaho senator William Borah instructed unhappy wets to undertake "faithful and patient" attempts to abide by the Eighteenth Amendment. Furious wets pointed out that prohibitionists, especially southern ones, had not been so careful to preserve enforcement of constitutional amendments that attempted to protect the civil and political rights of black southerners. "Governor [Al] Smith probably takes the same viewpoint of the Eighteenth Amendment," wrote one combative wet, "that the Governors of Georgia, Virginia, the Carolinas and other Southern States take regarding the Fourteenth and Fifteenth Amendments." Failure to enforce the Fourteenth Amendment, claimed New Jersey senator Edwards, set a precedent for ignoring the Eighteenth Amendment. "Does any rational human being in free America believe that the negro enjoys equality with the white—or that he ever will?" asked Edwards. "Like the Fourteenth Amendment, the Eighteenth has failed of execution. . . . It is a waste of time and money for an honest government to attempt to maintain such constitutional measures."[8]

The nullification argument failed to unite the wet resistance to the Eighteenth Amendment. For the anti-prohibitionist congressman George Tinkham, the abandonment of the Reconstruction amendments did not compare to the failure of prohibition. The Republican maverick, a supporter of African American rights, instead emphasized the obligation to enforce the Fourteenth Amendment. Experts cautioned against the dangers of constitutional nullification. The Harvard law professor and future Supreme Court justice Felix Frankfurter asked, "How many provisions of the Constitution can be flouted with impunity, without undue stress and strain on popular confidence in the Constitution, upon which the present social structure finally rests?" Most significantly for the eventual repeal of the Eighteenth Amendment, the AAPA, then emerging as the most responsible and influential anti-prohibition group, rejected nullification as damaging to social order and its conservative commitment to the rule of law.[9]

As prohibition efforts gained new vitality in the latter 1920s, so too did a better-coordinated and more purposeful anti-prohibition movement. As was the case with the passage and ratification of the Eighteenth Amendment, the successful movement for repeal arose from careful organization, focused leadership, and opportunity provided by unanticipated events. When the propitious moment arrived in 1932, the dismantling of the Eighteenth Amendment occurred even more quickly than had its speedy adoption between December 1917 and January 1919.

The AAPA developed the most effective constitutional critique of national prohibition. Officially organized in 1919 by William Stayton, a former naval officer, the AAPA contended that the Eighteenth Amendment violated fundamental American values of local self-government and limited federal authority. Prohibition, Stayton contended, "is a local question." In the early 1920s, several prominent business and political figures joined the APAA, among them John J. Raskob, of Du Pont and General Motors, brothers Irénée and Lammot Du Pont, of the giant chemical firm, and the financier Charles H. Sabin. Heightened concerns over taxation, expanding government power, and prohibition-induced lawlessness and corruption in 1926 drew even more influential figures into the AAPA, including Pierre Du Pont, ex–Packard Motors president Henry Bourne Joy, the wealthy former Republican senator from New York James W. Wadsworth Jr., and the brilliant, reactionary congressman and former US solicitor general James M. Beck.[10]

Deeply conservative in outlook, many of the AAPA's leading figures defined centralized government authority, rather than alcohol regulation in isolation, as a primary threat to traditional American patterns of governance and individual liberty. Stayton revealed that his activism was motivated as much by the movement for government regulation of child labor, by which "management of the family would be taken out of the control of parents," as it was by opposition to the Eighteenth Amendment. Wadsworth resisted federal action to grant suffrage to women by means of the Nineteenth Amendment as well as to enact prohibition through the Eighteenth. Years later, Raskob labeled the constitutional amendments for the direct election of senators, the income tax, women's suffrage, and the proposed child labor ban as, in each case, "a mistake." Pierre Du Pont maintained that the Eighteenth Amendment was an unconstitutional exercise of centralized power, because the amendment had not been approved by popular referenda. "It may be said emphatically," he stated in a 1929 radio address, "that the absolute prohibitions of the XVIIIth Amendment never received popular approval."[11] Of course, no amendment ever had received such treatment.

As the 1920s advanced and administrative centralization of prohibition enforcement improved, the defense of property against unwarranted government confiscation became more pronounced in AAPA statements. Pierre Du Pont, soon to become the dominant figure in the AAPA, expressed "outrage" in 1925 that the federal government had dismantled the liquor industry through the Eighteenth Amendment and the Volstead Act. "Much property invested in the production of alcoholic liquor, in a legal manner, was rendered useless, and there was no thought of recompense to the innocents who suffered," he objected. Although AAPA criticism of prohibition continued to detail the corrosive effects of law breaking, corruption, and loss of faith in institutions, increasingly the organization mounted an economic indictment of the prohibition regime. In 1928, the AAPA reorganized along business lines, with Pierre Du Pont assuming the chairmanship of a policymaking executive committee. Now upon a more secure financial footing, the AAPA launched a public-opinion campaign and established research and information departments to produce serious studies of the negative political, administrative, and economic consequences of prohibition, as well as promoting alternative systems of liquor control successfully employed in other nations. In an April resolution, the AAPA formally pledged to "work, first and foremost, for the entire repeal of the Eighteenth Amendment to the Constitution of the United States, to the end of casting out this solitary, sumptuary statute, the intrusion of which into constitutional realms has so severely hurt our country."[12]

ELITE LEADERSHIP OF A POPULAR MOVEMENT

Although the AAPA was capable and committed, it seemed unlikely that an elite association of business figures, high-society types, and conservative politicians could lead a popular movement to the unprecedented achievement of repealing an amendment to the Constitution. The historian David Kyvig stressed that the AAPA membership, which grew from 150,000 in 1930 to 550,000 in 1932, included many people of average means. On the other hand, the organization was top-heavy with inordinately wealthy and powerful individuals and did little to mask its arrogance and elitism. The AAPA did not acquire a common touch; instead, the economic and political landscape after 1928 altered dramatically in ways that allowed AAPA initiatives to more fully dovetail with popular criticism of prohibition.[13]

The Great Depression, for instance, transformed self-interested concerns about taxation into urgent demands for restoring industries, jobs, and government revenue. One of the frequent complaints of businesspeople in the AAPA was that the eradication of the liquor industry had removed significant tax revenue paid by liquor manufacturers and retailers to local and federal government. Increased corporate and personal taxes, several of them argued, made up for the lost liquor tax revenue. "The corporations of this country are being taxed 13% of their net profits, which is substantially in lieu of the tax on liquor which should flow to the Government," groused Irénée Du Pont in 1928. Reform of the Volstead Act or repeal of prohibition, printed AAPA materials suggested, would reduce or even eliminate income taxes. Hostile drys, such as Fletcher Dobyns in his 1940 arraignment of the repeal movement, concluded that the Du Ponts, Raskob, and company pursued repeal of prohibition in a selfish bid to lower their tax burden. The historian Daniel Okrent documented Pierre Du Pont's 1932 assessment that "repeal of the XVIIIth Amendment would permit Federal taxation in the amount of two billion dollars," which would "almost eliminate the income taxes of corporations and individuals."[14]

As David Kyvig has pointed out, however, most AAPA attention to the tax-revenue consequences of prohibition repeal was in the context of economic collapse after the crash. The need for jobs, economic stimulation, and tax revenue for government functions made the enforced idleness of the alcohol industry and its attendant businesses seem pointless to desperate Americans. AAPA research-department pamphlets, such as *Cost of Prohibition and Your Income Tax,* published in 1930, and *The Need of a New Source of Government Revenue,* issued in 1932, appeared during the desperate low point of the Depression. These reports addressed legitimate public-policy concerns, even if the resulting reforms also benefited the industrialists who supplied the information. The AAPA claimed that *Cost of Prohibition* attracted "nation-wide publicity and editorial endorsement," which "displeased" defenders of the Eighteenth Amendment.[15]

Other research pamphlets prepared by the AAPA reinforced popular resentment against misdeeds evident in prohibition enforcement. *Scandals of Prohibition Enforcement,* a serious study "based on Grand Jury disclosures" and a professional third-party investigation, handily illustrated the widespread corruption and misbehavior of the dry regime. *Reforming America with a Shotgun* chronicled the melancholy toll in human lives brought about by aggressive and often inept behavior by prohibition agents. The AAPA's report prompted a press survey that concluded that "more than 1,300 persons had been killed in the course of Prohibition enforcement." In both cases, material from the AAPA summed up the public mood of dissatisfaction with constitutional prohibition and energized demands for reform.[16]

Prior to the onset of the Depression, the institutional commitment to prohibition was secured by economic prosperity, the vigilant political lobby of the Anti-Saloon League, and the unwillingness of national political parties to take assertive positions on the dry experiment. Economic catastrophe and the ASL's loss of vitality allowed a repeal coalition to develop around the position staked out by the AAPA. Factionalism and lackluster leadership after the death of Wheeler, a Republican, loosened the ASL's grip on elected officials as the Depression deepened. Personal and financial scandals sidelined the league's most prominent Democrat, the Southern Methodist bishop James Cannon Jr., by 1930. The relentlessness of the Depression, rather than fear of the dry lobby, became the most powerful influence on the fate of prohibition.[17]

As the dry lobby faltered, new anti-prohibition organizations arose to challenge the Eighteenth Amendment. The most significant of these was the Women's Organization for National Prohibition Reform, formed in 1929 and led by Pauline Sabin, wife of the prominent AAPA member Charles Sabin. Pauline Sabin, a major figure among Republican women, had campaigned for Warren Harding in 1920, Calvin Coolidge in 1924, and Hoover in 1928. Hoover's commitment to enforcing prohibition, however, drove Sabin to resign from the Republican National Committee and become a repeal activist. Dry reformers had long assumed that prohibition attracted the support of the overwhelming majority of American women as a means to protect children, the family, and moral standards. The WONPR shattered that myth and developed a women's family-centered critique of prohibition. Beyond the infringement of local self-rule and economic costs emphasized by the AAPA, WONPR statements stressed "the shocking effect [prohibition] has had upon the youth of the nation." Official hypocrisy, corruption, crime, and excessive drinking, Sabin insisted, compelled young mothers to "work . . . for repeal because they don't want their babies to grow up in the hip-flask, speakeasy atmosphere that has polluted their own youth."[18]

Dry commentators struggled to portray Sabin and WONPR women as a female auxiliary to the elite AAPA. They were merely a "little group of wine-drinking society women," claimed Clarence True Wilson of the Methodist Board of Temperance. Sabin and other wealthy WONPR women shared connections with men in the AAPA, but the WONPR also reached into the ranks of ordinary Americans. The membership grew rapidly, until the WONPR claimed 1.5 million members at the end of 1933, which made the women's organization the largest anti-prohibition body in the United States. WONPR volunteers organized and electioneered in state-level repeal-referenda campaigns and in the ratification of the Twenty-First Amendment. As material conditions in the nation worsened, female activists broke the assumed ties between prohibition, the family, and the rights of women. Sabin went so far as to say, "I know of nothing since the days of the campaign for woman's suffrage to equal the campaign which women are now conducting for repeal of the Eighteenth Amendment."[19]

The legal profession and other respected associations joined in the institutional assault on the Eighteenth Amendment unleashed by hard times. A small group of New York attorneys critical of the Eighteenth Amendment formed the Volunteer Committee of Lawyers in early 1929. Chaired by AAPA member Joseph H. Choate Jr., the VCL argued that the Eighteenth Amendment unconstitutionally increased federal power over the rights of citizens and the states. Prodded by VCL attorneys, several city and state bar associations issued statements endorsing the return of liquor control to state governments. In late 1930, the American Bar Association by a two-to-one margin favored repeal of the Eighteenth Amendment in a referendum on prohibition. By 1931 the American Federation of Labor, the American Legion, and the Veterans of Foreign Wars had taken an anti-prohibition stand. Most of these groups endorsed state-level referenda to determine whether prohibition should be repealed or modified. Public-opinion polls and state referenda suggested that popular toleration for prohibition was running out. When AAPA president Henry Curran remarked in 1931 that "Americans are sick, as never before, of the squandering of millions of dollars on an exploded experiment while people are clamoring for work and food," he spoke not only for conservative industrialists but for increasing numbers of ordinary Americans as well.[20]

Beginning in 1928, the refusal of the major parties to articulate meaningful positions on prohibition gradually ended, thus opening the way to repeal. Mindful of ASL lobbyists and their own wet and dry factions, Democrats and Republicans issued carefully noncommittal appeals to law enforcement in 1920s party platforms. Al Smith's nomination as the Democratic candidate for president in 1928 began the process by which Democrats came to be associated with repeal, and Republicans with continued attempts to enforce the Eighteenth Amendment. Yet while Smith was wet, his running mate, Joseph Robinson, of Arkansas, was dry, and the party platform tilted modestly toward enforcement. Although Smith lost badly in the 1928 election, that same year the New Yorker appointed John J. Raskob, an AAPA stalwart, as chairman of the

Democratic National Committee. Raskob, a former Republican, and his deputy, Jouett Shouse, a former dry, worked over the next four years to commit the Democrats to a "home-rule" amendment empowering individual states to opt out of national prohibition. In keeping with AAPA demands that prohibition be subjected to a vote of the people, the proposed amendment suggested that each state determine by popular referendum whether it would assume alcohol regulation within its borders.[21]

Republicans, on the other hand, were ensnared by Hoover's effort to enforce prohibition and his inability to combat the Depression. Attempts by GOP wets to modify the party's position on the Eighteenth Amendment were rebuffed by Hoover loyalists. Deteriorating economic conditions doomed Hoover to defeat in 1932. The Democrats, by contrast, endorsed outright repeal in 1932. The Democratic nominee, Franklin Roosevelt, was hostile to Raskob and cautious on repeal, but he embraced the will of the convention with his usual pragmatic enthusiasm. Voters swept Roosevelt into office, along with a wet majority in Congress. Rather than waiting for the new Congress to convene in March 1933, the lame-duck session, which featured a stronger wet contingent than any previous prohibition-era Congress, enacted a repeal amendment by wide majorities in February. The proposed Twenty-First Amendment flatly repealed the Eighteenth Amendment and stipulated that ratification occur by means of state conventions. Shortly before passage of the new amendment, the VCL's Choate supplied a model bill to governors and state legislatures detailing procedures for electing delegates and organizing ratification conventions. Aided by anti-prohibition groups, most states rapidly developed convention mechanisms, elected delegates between April and November, and convened conventions, many of which immediately voted to ratify the Twenty-First Amendment. On December 5, 1933, the Twenty-First Amendment was ratified (the onetime dry stronghold of Utah taking the honors as the thirty-sixth state to ratify), and prohibition was repealed. Without careful organization and the desperate circumstances stemming from the Depression, repeal on so fundamental a scale at such a swift pace would not have happened.[22]

The repeal of the Eighteenth Amendment made certain that Americans would remember national prohibition as a failed policy, but that widespread acknowledgment of prohibition's shortcomings by itself produced repeal is a myth. As we have seen, many expert contemporary observers, both drys and wets, believed that prohibition would remain part of the Constitution. Drys hoped that means could be found to better enforce the unchanging law of the land. For their part, wets worked to construct a mild enforcement regime that would soften the impossible demands of constitutional prohibition. It took the Great Depression, the economic equivalent of a natural disaster, to reshape the landscape of possibilities and open a path to repeal. The Depression shattered the rosy predictions of prohibition's economic benefits and lay bare the cost in lost jobs, shuttered industries, and uncollected tax revenue attributable to the dry reform. Repeal still would not have happened without interest groups such as the AAPA, the WONPR, and the VCL, which shaped public opinion for repeal, framed repeal policies and won support for them in the Democratic Party, and fashioned workable mechanisms by which the repeal amendment could be ratified by popular opinion. Opportunity, organization, and political drive ended prohibition; general dissatisfaction with the dry regime did not.

NOTES

1. W. J. Rorabaugh, "Alcohol, Consumption of, per Capita (United States)," in *Alcohol and Temperance in Modern History: An International Encyclopedia,* ed. Jack S. Blocker Jr., David M. Fahey, and Ian R. Tyrrell, vol. 1 (Santa Barbara, CA: ABC-CLIO, 2003), 23–24; W. J. Rorabaugh, *The Alcoholic Republic: An American Tradition* (New York: Oxford University Press, 1979), 233; Perry R. Duis, *The Saloon: Public Drinking in Chicago and Boston, 1880–1920* (Urbana: University of Illinois Press, 1983); David E. Kyvig, *Repealing National Prohibition,* 2nd ed. (Kent, OH: Kent State University Press, 2000), 58; William Dickmeyer, Allen County Death Records, Allen County Genealogical Society of Indiana.

2. National Commission on Law Observance and Enforcement, *Report on the Enforcement of the Prohibition Laws of the United States* (Washington, DC: US Government Printing Office, 1931), 21.

3. Kyvig, *Repealing National Prohibition,* 34; Clarence Darrow, "The Ordeal of Prohibition," *American Mercury* 2 (August 1924): 419; Irving Fisher, *Prohibition at Its Worst* (New York: Macmillan, 1926), 227.

4. Jesse Tarbert, "When Good Government Meant Big Government: Nationalism, Racism, and the Quest to Strengthen the American State, 1918–1933" (PhD diss., Case Western Reserve University, 2016), 116–34.

5. Lisa McGirr, *The War on Alcohol: Prohibition and the Rise of the American State* (New York: Norton, 2016), 189–203; National Commission on Law Observance and Enforcement, *Report*, 83.

6. Kyvig, *Repealing National Prohibition*, 15–19, 33–35; Thomas R. Pegram, "Prohibition," in *The American Congress: The Building of Democracy*, ed. Julian E. Zelizer (Boston: Houghton Mifflin, 2004), 424–25; Daniel Okrent, *Last Call: The Rise and Fall of Prohibition* (New York: Scribner, 2010), 229–32, 266–70.

7. Okrent, *Last Call*, 257–61; Gilman M. Ostrander, *The Prohibition Movement in California, 1848–1933* (Berkeley: University of California Press, 1957), 150, 172; Michael A. Lerner, *Dry Manhattan: Prohibition in New York City* (Cambridge, MA: Harvard University Press, 2007), 93–95; Arthur Twining Hadley, "Law Making and Law Enforcement," *Harper's Magazine* 151 (November 1925): 645; Walter Lippmann, "Our Predicament under the Eighteenth Amendment," *Harper's Magazine* 154 (December 1926): 56; Kyvig, *Repealing National Prohibition*, 66–67.

8. "Fears City Will Be Bootleg Rendezvous," *New York Times*, 7 May 1923, 4; Gifford Pinchot, "Why I Believe in Enforcing the Prohibition Laws," *Annals of the American Academy of Political and Social Science* 109 (September 1923): 284; "Challenges Borah on Nullification; Edwards Disputes the Alleged Statement That 14th and 15th Amendments are Upheld," *New York Times*, 17 June 1926, 3; C. B. Squire, "The Other Amendments," *New York Times*, 1 July 1923, xx8. See also, William L. Fish, "Other Amendments Not Enforced," *New York Times*, 22 May 1925, 18.

9. "Negro Right to Vote Is Urged on Harding," *New York Times*, 4 December 1922, 2; Felix Frankfurter, "A National Policy for Enforcement of Prohibition," *Annals of the American Academy of Political and Social Science* 109 (September 1923): 193; Kyvig, *Repealing National Prohibition*, 67.

10. *Who, How, Why of the Association Against the Prohibition Amendment* (AAPA pamphlet, 30 November 1929), reprinted in *Official Records of the National Commission on Law Observance and Enforcement*, vol. 5 (Washington, DC: Government Printing Office, 1931), 275–86; Kyvig, *Repealing National Prohibition*, 43 (Stayton), 49, 73–78; Morton Keller, *In Defense of Yesterday: James M. Beck and the Politics of Conservatism* (New York: Coward-McCann, 1958), 209–10.

11. Kyvig, *Repealing National Prohibition*, 43, 76; Okrent, *Last Call*, 332; Pierre S. Du Pont, "A Business Man's View of Prohibition," 5 December 1929, reprinted in *Official Records of the National Commission*, 5:310.

12. Kyvig, *Repealing National Prohibition*, 82, 92–93, 97.

13. Kyvig, *Repealing National Prohibition*, 95–96; Okrent, *Last Call*, 333.

14. Kyvig, *Repealing National Prohibition*, 79; Okrent, *Last Call*, 332–33; Fletcher Dobyns, *The Amazing Story of Repeal: An Expose of the Power of Propaganda* (Chicago: Willett, Clark, 1940), 19–26, 52.

15. Kyvig, *Repealing National Prohibition*, 131–33; *Annual Report of the Association Against the Prohibition Amendment*, 15 January 1930, reprinted in *Official Records of the National Commission*, 5:330.

16. *Annual Report*, 329–30, 332.

17. K. Austin Kerr, *Organized for Prohibition: A New History of the Anti-Saloon League* (New Haven, CT: Yale University Press, 1985), 239–41; Okrent, *Last Call*, 300–302; Robert A. Hohner, *Prohibition and Politics: The Life of Bishop James Cannon, Jr.* (Columbia: University of South Carolina Press, 1999), 242–75.

18. Kenneth D. Rose, *American Women and the Repeal of Prohibition* (New York: New York University Press, 1996), 11; Kyvig, *Repealing National Prohibition*, 118–23 (Sabin, 122).

19. Rose, *American Women*, 79–83 (Wilson, 83), 96–101, 107–8; Kyvig, *Repealing National Prohibition*, 123; Lerner, *Dry Manhattan*, 197.

20. Kyvig, *Repealing National Prohibition*, 116–17, 127–29, 133 (Curran), 134–35; John G. Gebhart, "Movement Against Prohibition," *Annals of the American Academy of Political and Social Science* 163 (September 1932): 172–73, 177–78, 180.

21. Douglas B. Craig, *After Wilson: The Struggle for the Democratic Party, 1920–1934* (Chapel Hill: University of North Carolina Press, 1992), 187–93; Kyvig, *Repealing National Prohibition*, 144–46.

22. Gebhart, "Movement Against Prohibition," 179; Craig, *After Wilson*, 244; Kyvig, *Repealing National Prohibition*, 153–58, 168–82.

PROHIBITION WAS UNIQUELY AMERICAN

MARK LAWRENCE SCHRAD

"There is no social movement in our day more amazing than the world-wide rebellion against rum domination," claimed A. C. Archibald in December 1915—more than a year before the United States joined the "great war" that had already engulfed Europe. "Who would have dreamed that autocratic Russia would so soon become a prohibition nation? Whiskey-ridden England . . . France, and even Germany, have taken steps to check the liquor traffic," the American reverend Archibald said. Closer to home, "Canada has outlawed the saloon from a number of her provinces. Newfoundland voted dry at an election last month. In our own country eighty per cent of the territory is dry and sixty-five per cent of the people are living in districts where the saloon is no longer tolerated." To have belligerent and nonbelligerent nations alike all moving against the liquor traffic was perhaps a small silver lining in a terrible war. "What is the basis of this world-wide phenomena? Such world movements were never built on sand foundations."[1]

To be sure, the United States was not the only country to undertake a "noble experiment" with alcohol prohibition. Many countries did. But figuring out exactly how many requires that we first define what we mean by *prohibition.*

WHAT "COUNTS" AS PROHIBITION?

The reverend's words are a time capsule of both the opportunities and the challenges that come from looking at alcohol prohibition beyond the borders of the United States. While we still commonly think of both temperance and prohibition as uniquely American phenomena, they were not. Efforts to combat the drink traffic can be found throughout the history of most countries on earth, becoming increasingly woven into a transnational temperance-advocacy network beginning in the mid-nineteenth century, especially across Europe and North America.[2] Still, looking abroad to address even the most basic question—what counts as alcohol prohibition?—is tinged by the American experience.

For one, as Archibald points out, many of the belligerent countries of Europe enacted dramatic restrictions on alcohol during World War I, from increased taxes and curtailed sales hours to rations or bans on specific beverages. But since some did not dive headlong into the most draconian option—full, statutory prohibition—does that count as prohibition? The severity of the anti-alcohol restrictions varies, and seems to matter. Iceland had what we would consider prohibition beginning in 1915. But wine was legalized in 1922 and distilled spirits in 1933. Beer with over a 2.25 percent alcohol content was prohibited in Iceland until 1989, so when did "prohibition" end in Iceland?

Second, as Archibald also points out, by 1915 some 80 percent of the United States had gone "dry" by enacting the local option at the county level or banning the liquor traffic at the state level. Does that count? After all, what are dry counties—like those that still dot the American South—but mini-prohibitions? With the notable exception of Quebec, most Canadian provinces enacted prohibition legislation. Does that make Canada a "prohibition country"? Apparently, the territorial scope of the prohibition seems to matter.

What about temporary, "emergency" prohibitions? In 1909, labor unions in Sweden pushed forward with a general strike. In anticipation of drunken disorder, unions and factory owners all implored the crown to decree a prohibition. The government conceded and banned the sale of alcoholic beverages for the duration of the (largely peaceful) nation-wide strike. The strike lasted exactly one month, and so too did the prohibition. Does that count? Obviously, the duration of the prohibition matters. But what about emergency bans during World War I, which were only intended to last the duration of the war?

The Brussels International Conference of 1889 outlawed both the international slave trade and the liquor traffic in vast swaths of colonial Africa.[3] In North America, Native Americans were legally prohibited from buying alcohol from 1682 in Pennsylvania and as early as 1633 in the New Netherland and Massachusetts Bay colonies.[4] Does it count as prohibition if the decision is imposed by an outside, colonial force or applies only to a specific segment of the population? Then what about New Zealand? A majority (but not a supermajority) of Kiwis voted in favor of nationwide dry laws, but they had to settle for a patchwork of no-license districts. Does that count? Whether the prohibition reflects the "will of the people" certainly varies, though it is unclear whether that matters when defining prohibition.

Finally, what about the swath of Muslim-majority countries from Libya to Saudi Arabia to Pakistan to Indonesia that have nationwide prohibitions on alcohol to this day? Do we count those? Both the time frame and the dynamics seem different than what we're used to in regard to American prohibition, but if we admit that prohibition had some foundation in organized religion, how can we justify including prohibitions pushed by midwestern evangelical protestants but not those pushed by Middle Eastern Sunni Muslims?

This is just a brief introduction to the world of complexity beyond the American experience. Still, we need to define some boundaries. For the purposes of this chapter, I will consider only those cases of nation-wide, statutory prohibition of both distilled and fermented beverages undertaken by sovereign, self-governing states, of at least three months' duration, before the onset of World War II. This excludes consideration of local option and subnational "prohibitions," temporary emergency measures, partial prohibitions of a certain type of beverage, colonial impositions, and the more "modern" prohibitions in postcolonial, Muslim-majority states. Of course, different definitions will lead to the inclusion or exclusion of different ranges of cases, but for the purposes of this brief chapter, these limits produce a reasonable number of cases that largely conform to what we conventionally envision prohibition to look like based on the American experience.

Based on these criteria, I count eleven prohibition countries beyond the United States. We will begin by examining the Russian Empire/early Soviet Union, as well as those cases influenced by the Russian experience—Hungary, Finland, and Estonia. We then turn to the countries of the North Atlantic—Belgium, Iceland, Norway, Canada, and Newfoundland— before concluding with Turkey and British India.

RUSSIAN EMPIRE/SOVIET UNION, 1914-1925

In his 1915 statement, Reverend Archibald seemed to be most incredulous that the Russian Empire would become the world's first prohibition nation. Perhaps that is because in the American experience the precondition to prohibition was a robust temperance movement, whereas autocratic Russia had long banned temperance organizations "lest they be mistaken for separate religious sects."[5] What's more, more than one-third of the revenues of the mighty tsarist empire originated from the imperial retail monopoly on vodka. With the entire imperial autocracy built upon promoting the drunken misery of its people, no genuine, grass-roots sobriety movement could ever hope to succeed: "If temperance were to succeed, the Russian state would fail—it was as simple as that."[6]

Still, Russia became the first prohibition nation as a result of the inept leadership of Tsar Nicholas II. A heavy drinker in his youth, Nicholas had gradually been won to the cause of temperance, largely by members of the royal family. The tsar's "dearest uncle Kostya"—Grand Duke Konstantin Konstantinovich Romanov—made frequent temperance admonishments to his beloved little "Niki." Even the notoriously debauching Siberian mystic, Grigory Rasputin, argued that "it is unbefitting for a

Tsar to deal in vodka and make drunkards out of honest people. . . . The time has come to lock up the Tsar's saloons."[7] By January 1914 Tsar Nicholas appeared to be a full convert to temperance, appointing a new finance minister, Pyotr Lvovich Bark, whom he charged with no longer making "the treasury dependent on the ruination of the spiritual and economic forces of the majority of My faithful subjects."[8]

Upon being drawn into World War I in the summer of 1914, Russia followed the conventional wisdom of the tsar's cousin Kaiser Wilhelm II—that victory in the next war would go to the most sober—by declaring prohibition in those areas actively being mobilized for war.[9] Much of this cult of military sobriety was aimed at avoiding Russia's painful experiences of riotous mobs at conscription points and scenes of drunken soldiers stumbling to their slaughter during the disastrous Russo-Japanese War (1904–5). And while the Russian archives include reams of reports of drunken riots, the tsar and the high command apparently received only glowing news of patriotism in full bloom, surging labor productivity, and a remarkably smooth and sober call-up that allowed for the deployment of troops in half the time expected.[10] Meanwhile, Finance Minister Bark reported that the loss of any vodka revenues could easily be replaced with a slapdash mix of war bonds, foreign loans, and miscellaneous taxes. The tsar was pleased.

Yet this was at best a partial prohibition, as it only covered military districts and did not touch the hotels and restaurants of the well-to-do aristocracy. That all changed in September 1914, when Prince Oleg Konstantinovich Romanov was killed in battle on the Lithuanian front, the only Romanov to die in military service in World War I. As a symbolic gesture to Prince Oleg's grieving father—and the tsar's favorite uncle, Kostya—Nicholas II telegrammed Grand Duke Konstantin Konstantinovich that "I have already decided to abolish forever the government sale of vodka in Russia."[11]

Russian prohibition was, if anything, far more disastrous than anything experienced in the United States. Certainly there were some temporary improvements in popular sobriety, but nothing that would produce the near-miraculous upsurge in productivity and national moral rejuvenation that temperance advocates had hoped for and policymakers were relying on. Indeed, prohibition hastened the downfall of the tsarist regime itself.[12] First, prohibition fed popular discontent with the tsarist system. No matter how benevolent his intention, the tsar's prohibition decree did little to win him support from his people. As contemporaries noted, "The population could not stand forced abstinence," which not only heightened discontent with the imperial leadership but also led to drinking dangerous home brews, eau de cologne, shoe polish, lacquers, and varnishes. After just a few months of prohibition, "dry" Russia was inundated with a wave of alcohol poisonings.[13] Still, it takes more than discontent with being forced to go cold turkey to make a revolution.

Second, prohibition exacerbated the wartime infrastructural paralysis. Russia is a vast country with an inhospitable climate. When its brutal winters gave way to the spring thaw and soaking rains, the empire's network of dirt roads turned to mud, becoming virtually impassable. Russia's railway infrastructure, then in its infancy, was incapable of adequately supplying armies at the front and maintaining the traditional urban-rural trade cycle that transported grain to the cities and manufactured goods to the countryside. Since they could no longer sell their vodka to the tsar's retail monopoly thanks to prohibition, many wealthy, aristocratic distillers packed Russia's limited rolling stock with alcohol bound for the Arctic ports of Murmansk and Arkhangelsk for a long sea voyage to markets in France or even across the single-rail Trans-Siberian Railway to China and Japan.[14] In the meantime, demoralized armies on the German and Austro-Hungarian fronts went without supplies, leading to mass insubordination and desertion, and angry workers in beleaguered cities like Moscow and Petrograd went without food, leading to strikes, riots, and revolution.

Finally, and most importantly, the imperial vodka monopoly was the single largest contributor to the imperial treasury, accounting for around one-third of all state income. With prohibition the vodka revenues all but ceased, just as Russia was mobilizing some 12 million men into the largest army the world had ever seen. Even then, in 1915, an imperial finance report actively boasted that "never since the dawn of human history has a single country, in a time of war, renounced the principal source of its revenue."[15] There is a reason for that.

Even with a band-aid mix of taxes, Russian state revenues declined by more than 500 million rubles in the second half of 1914 and by 900 million rubles per year thereafter, largely owing to the loss of alcohol sales.[16] "What if we do lose eight hundred million rubles in revenue?" Premier Ivan Goremykin mused dismissively. "We shall print that much paper money; it's all the same to the people."[17] Largely unaware of modern macroeconomic principles, Russia patched the budgetary hole with newly printed rubles, leading to a hyperinflationary spiral that made the currency worthless. Hyperinflation fanned the flames of popular discontent that dethroned the tsar in the February Revolution of 1917 and unseated his successor, the Provisional Government, in the Bolshevik Revolution in October 1917.[18]

Despite the revolutionary transition from Europe's most conservative autocracy to the world's first communist state, alcohol prohibition and grain requisitioning were the only policies continued by both regimes. For the Bolsheviks, the tsar's ill-fated prohibition was a useful inheritance. Whether in Siberian prisons or in European exile, Vladimir Lenin for decades had been lambasting the tsarist vodka monopoly as the foremost specimen of tsarist capitalism's "predatory economy," in which the rich got richer off the drunken misery of the masses.[19] He was not wrong. "The proletariat as a rising class does not need drunkenness that would deafen or provoke them," the revolutionary prohibitionist Lenin proclaimed in 1901. "They need only clarity, clarity, and again clarity. The communist upbringing of the working class requires the rooting-out of all vestiges of the capitalist past, especially such a dangerous vestige as drunkenness."[20]

After the Bolsheviks seized power in Petrograd, their opposition to vodka became a matter of life and death. With only a tenuous grasp on power, Lenin rightly worried that the new regime could be toppled by drunken pogroms. To maintain order in Petrograd, they organized a secret-police force—the Extraordinary Commission for Combatting Counter-Revolution and Sabotage, or CheKa, which would later become the NKVD and then the KGB—to root out alcohol. Alcohol stocks in the capital would be blown up with dynamite. Bootleggers would be shot on sight.[21] Still, despite such draconian penalties, Russians continued to drink.

By the early 1920s the Red Army had secured some modicum of security for the new regime in a brutal and multi-front civil war against the royalist "white" forces. Despite ongoing famine, the economy was showing signs of life under Lenin's strategic concession to capitalist principles, the New Economic Policy (NEP). Still, drunkenness was rampant in the countryside, and the Bolsheviks were powerless to do anything about it. The Soviets stepped up raids against illegal distillers, but moonshining was so widespread that these shock campaigns were like "shooting a cannon at sparrows."[22] Lenin was pragmatic with his NEP concessions to the market. Nevertheless, even as he was laid low by a series of strokes that would soon claim his life, in 1922 Lenin remained absolute when it came to prohibition: "I think that we should not follow the example of the capitalist countries and put vodka and other intoxicants on the market, because, profitable though they are, they will lead us back to capitalism and not forward to communism."[23]

As Lenin's health faded, so too did his control. Beer and wine had been legalized in 1922 but did little to stem the tide of homemade vodka flooding the countryside. And while some members of the old guard, like Leon Trotsky, remained resolute defenders of prohibition, they were already being outmaneuvered by Joseph Stalin. On October 1, 1925, with Lenin dead and Stalin consolidating power, the Soviets officially repealed the failed, decade-long experiment with prohibition, resurrecting the old vodka monopoly, but emblazoned with the hammer and the sickle. Within a few short years, vodka would regain its place as the primary source of revenue for the new Soviet superpower. Asking "which is better: enslavement to foreign capital or the introduction of vodka?" Stalin later conceded: "Naturally, we decided on vodka, because we figured that if we had to dirty our hands a little for the cause of the victory of the proletariat and the peasantry, we would resort even to this extreme in the interest of our cause."[24]

HUNGARY, 1919

In the waning months of World War I, the once formidable Austro-Hungarian Empire was collapsing upon itself, with the South Slavs, the Romanians, the Poles, the Ukrainians, the Czechs, and the Slovaks all clamoring for self-determination. Residents of the newly established (1918) Hungarian Republic became increasingly incensed as the victorious Allied powers demanded ever more territorial concessions—some 70 percent of the old Kingdom of Hungary—to these newly formed neighboring states. With promises that Lenin and Bolshevik Russia would help Hungary restore their former borders, Hungarian communists led by Béla Kun seized control of the state, declaring the establishment of the Hungarian Soviet Republic on March 21, 1919.

While Russian military assistance never materialized, Kun maintained constant radiotelegraph communication with Lenin and proclaimed Hungary to be legally part of the new Bolshevik state, despite being separated from Moscow by more than a thousand miles. Taking his cues from the Kremlin, Kun instituted brutal Soviet-style policies, including nationalization of industry, collectivization of agriculture, gunpoint grain requisitioning, and prohibition of alcohol in the traditionally wine-growing region—all of which led to inflation and food shortages and undermined support for the new regime in the countryside.[25] Hungary's communist experiment collapsed on August 1, 1919, as the communists were driven out of Budapest with the help of the Romanians. Béla Kun fled to Red Vienna and then Moscow, where he would later die as a victim of a Stalinist purge. Still, for its entire 133 days of existence, the Hungarian Soviet Republic was nominally a prohibition country.

FINLAND, 1914–1931

Lenin and the Bolsheviks were not the only ones happy with the tsar's prohibitionist legacy. The Grand Duchy of Finland had been an autonomous region of the Russian Empire since the Napoleonic Wars. While legislation of the Finnish Diet needed the assent of the tsar, there was more freedom of organization in Finland than in Russia proper, which—like Scandinavia generally—had a robust temperance movement. The Finns had passed prohibition bills in 1907 and 1909, but because of alcohol's centrality to the Russian Empire's finances, neither received imperial promulgation. Only in May 1917, months after the February Revolution toppled the tsar, did Russia's new Provisional Government promulgate the law.[26] But by then the Finns, as subjects of the Russian Empire, had already been under the tsar's blanket prohibition since 1914—though its enforcement was haphazard at best, owing to the exigencies of war.[27]

According to the bill, Finland would be dry beginning June 1, 1919, but by then much had changed. When the Bolsheviks took power in Petrograd, they declared a general right of self-determination for the peoples of Russia on November 15, 1917. The same day, Finland declared its independence, setting off a brief, though bloody, civil war between communist reds and anti-socialist whites in 1918. The whites won.

Still, in form, duration, and dynamics, Finland's "noble experiment" (1919–31) most closely resembles the American experience. Like its American counterpart, Finnish prohibition was aimed at the liquor traffic, banning not the consumption of alcohol but the import, manufacture, and sale of beverages containing more than 2 percent alcohol by volume. According to contemporaries, penalties for infractions consisted mostly of "ridiculously small" fines and only occasionally very brief jail time.[28] Enforcement was inconsistent at best, with oversight divided among police, the Customs Guard, and volunteers. Finland's long, meandering, sparsely populated Baltic coastline made smuggling far more of a problem than illegal moonshining.

Also like American prohibition Finnish prohibition endured until the 1930s, despite ever-growing public opposition. In both 1922 and 1931, the government appointed special committees to study the liquor question, and both times they endorsed continuing prohibition, despite mass anti-prohibition protests, repeal planks for all major political parties, and unofficial polls suggesting that some 90 percent of Finns wanted repeal. By 1932—in the midst of the global Great Depression—the liquor question had become such a political hot potato that it was put to a nationwide referendum. With more than 70 percent of the country voting in favor of repeal, the parliament was called into special session to bring Finland's thirteen-year experiment with prohibition to an end.[29]

ESTONIA, 1914–1920

Like Finland, Estonia was subject to the tsar's prohibition from the very beginning of the World War I in 1914. In the borderlands between the German Empire and Russia proper, the Baltic region felt the full brunt of war and the associated military restrictions on alcohol. Still, with the collapse of tsarism in February 1917, enforcement of Nicholas's prohibition all but ended, as moonshining and illegal distilleries proliferated. Revolution was accompanied by mass desertion at the front, allowing Germany to advance rapidly across Estonia. Following the retreat of Russian forces, Estonia declared its independence on February 24, 1918, before being overrun and occupied by advancing Germans. Following the Treaty of Brest-Litovsk in March 1918, which formally ended the war on the eastern front, the Germans retreated and the Bolsheviks renounced all claims to the Baltic States, with political authority reverting to the Provisional Estonian Government.

Unlike neighboring Latvia and Lithuania, which were still grappling with competing claims of sovereignty, the new Estonian government maintained the legal code of the old Russian Empire. This meant that the tsar's prohibition decree remained formally the law of independent Estonia for another two years, as the country battled a war of independence (1918–20) against the westward encroachments of the Bolshevik Red Army.

The Constituent Assembly legalized the alcohol trade on April 27, 1920. Brewers and distillers hoped that Estonia could build a burgeoning liquor trade and smuggle their wares into the nearby "dry" territories of

Finland and the Soviet Union, but amid war, famine, and reconstruction those plans were largely unrealized.[30]

BELGIUM, 1914–1918

Before the war, Belgium had the second-highest alcohol consumption in Europe (after France). Boasting a robust civil society, Belgium was also the seat of a growing, transnational temperance community. But with the outbreak of hostilities, King Albert prohibited the sale of beer, wine, and liquors in the territory occupied by Belgian or Allied troops and said that "prohibition should be extended to other Belgian territory as fast as it should be liberated."[31]

Of course, thanks to the Schlieffen Plan, Germany did an end run around French fortifications by invading through neutral Belgium and Luxembourg, which then drew Britain into the war. Consequently, some 90 percent of Belgium was occupied by German forces. Following the kaiser's instructions, Germany had its own, stringent restrictions against distilled liquors but was more permissive toward wine and beer.

On Armistice Day, November 11, 1918, Belgium reaffirmed its prohibition against distilled spirits as an emergency measure to maintain public order. While restrictions against Belgian beers and wines were gradually lifted, the prohibition of distilled liquor—Vandervelde's Law, as it was known, after the temperate Social Democratic leader Emile Vandervelde—would remain in place for most of the twentieth century, as the Belgian alcohol market would become one of the most heavily regulated in Europe.[32]

ICELAND, 1915–1922

A country of some 340,000 inhabitants on a volcanic island in the North Atlantic, Iceland is one of Europe's smaller and more remote countries.

Iceland gained home rule from Denmark in 1904, with sovereignty over domestic affairs, ultimately gaining full sovereignty following World War I in 1918.

Iceland has a rich history of prohibition. As in other Scandinavian countries, in Iceland temperance activism was strong, leading the parliament (Alþingi) to introduce a blanket prohibition on the sale of alcoholic beverages in 1915.[33] This prohibition fell victim to a trade war with Spain, which threatened to close its market to Iceland's primary export, cod, unless Iceland allowed the importation of Spanish wines. In 1922, Iceland relented and began permitting the importation of wine from Spain. In an advisory referendum in 1933, 58 percent of Icelandic voters voted to repeal prohibition, which was accomplished in 1935, with one glaring omission: strong beer, with an alcohol content above 2.25 percent, would remain banned. (As in many European countries, light beers and pilsners with less than 2.25 percent alcohol are often regarded as nonalcoholic and are not as strenuously regulated.)

Still, between 1935 and 1988 more than twenty attempts were made before the Alþingi to repeal the beer ban, failing each time in the face of persistent arguments that beer would essentially become a "gateway drug" to heavier drinking by Icelandic youth. Only in 1989 did Iceland finally liberalize its peculiar beer ban and remove the last vestiges of prohibition.[34]

NORWAY, 1916-1927

In 1905, following an amicable dissolution of its union with Sweden, Norway became an independent country. Norway was nominally neutral in World War I. Much of Norway's merchant marine supported the country's traditional trade ties with Great Britain and was decimated by German U-boat campaigns. Along with a robust temperance movement, the Norwegian liquor traffic was strenuously regulated; Norway adopted the Swedish "Gothenburg system" of municipal control, with some regions effectively voting themselves dry through local option.

Still, a royal edict ordered that the sales of spiritous liquors and wines were to be prohibited for the holiday season from December 18, 1916, to January 8, 1917. The impacts of the sudden prohibition were so remarkable that temperance advocates continued to push for its continuance through Stortung (parliament) legislation throughout 1918, when it was extended to beer with above 2.5 percent alcohol.[35]

Following the conclusion of the war, in 1919, Norway's first nationwide plebiscite was held, an advisory referendum returning 62 percent of voters in favor of making prohibition permanent.[36] But the government had difficulty translating the will of the voters into legislation. As with Iceland and other, smaller European states, much of Norway's domestic politics and economics was intimately dependent upon securing amicable trade relations with its more powerful partners. This time, not just Spain but France and Portugal too wanted to export wines to "dry" Norway in exchange for cod. With the Norwegian economy hanging in the balance, in 1923 the Stortung relented and permitted the importation of wines from these countries while still maintaining a prohibition against beer and liquor.

Not surprisingly, with its extensive coastline of rugged fjords, Norway's prohibition was bedeviled by extensive smuggling in addition to illicit domestic distilling. With increasing arrests for drunkenness highlighting the shortcomings of the policy, by the mid-1920s (as in Finland and Sweden) prohibition had become such a political lightning rod—threatening to tear parties along wet/dry lines—that the issue was again put to the people through a nationwide referendum. The 1926 vote returned a 56 percent majority favoring repeal. When the repeal took effect on April 4, 1927, liquor sales were restored in government shops in just thirteen cities across Norway.[37]

CANADA, 1918–1920

Canada is a difficult country to code in terms of prohibition, both because it was a British dominion—somewhere between a colony and a sovereign state—and because liquor control was largely relegated to the provincial level. In 1867, the colony of Canada entered into a confederation with New Brunswick and Nova Scotia to become the de facto self-governing country of Canada (though its formal independence from Britain wouldn't be recognized until 1931, if not 1982). Still, Canada did have a robust temperance community, led by the Dominion Alliance for the Total Suppression of the Liquor Traffic, established in 1877.[38] The following year, the Canada Temperance Act (Scott Act) was passed in Ottawa, allowing any locality to outlaw the liquor trade with a bare-majority vote.[39]

Prince Edward Island was the pioneer of Canadian prohibition, voting itself dry in 1901. The rest of the Canadian provinces enacted prohibition only after Canada—as a British dominion—declared war against Germany in 1914. The notable exception was Quebec, whose urban areas consistently opposed prohibition. This put Quebec in a strange place, as in 1918 Ottawa declared a wartime prohibition on any beverage with an alcohol content of more than 2.5 percent by volume, to endure one year beyond the conclusion of the war.[40] We can thus consider a nationwide prohibition in Canada lasting only until 1920, with Quebec abandoning it at the first opportunity, followed by the Yukon Territory. Most Canadian provinces repealed their blanket prohibitions during the mid-1920s, with, again, the noteworthy exception of Prince Edward Island, which only legalized the alcohol trade in 1948.

NEWFOUNDLAND, 1917–1924

Special mention must be made here of Newfoundland, another British dominion, which would not become part of Canada proper until 1949. In 1915 the sparsely populated maritime state voted 80–20 percent in favor of prohibition. "Our people have never been what one could call a drinking people," wrote Sir Wilfred Thomason Grenfell in 1921, extolling the virtues of prohibition—noting that the French speakers along the Gulf of St. Lawrence drank more than the rest. "Occasionally I have seized a schooner running an illicit supply but never had any serious trouble. In protection of our women, in provision for our children, in better thrift and in every possible way our coast has benefitted by Prohibition," he claimed. "I have had one or two trivial cases of moonshining, but it is not extensively carried on."[41] Even Grenfell later had to admit that the prohibition law was easily avoided by pharmacists selling liquor prescriptions or by potential purchasers directly lobbying the public controller.

Following the wave of repeal sentiment across the entire North Atlantic in the 1920s, Newfoundland repealed its prohibition in 1924, replacing it with a system of municipal liquor control like those in Quebec and Scandinavia, limiting purchase to only one bottle of distilled spirits per day, but placing no restrictions on the sale of fermented wines and beers.

TURKEY, 1920–1924

Just as we must be careful not to portray prohibition simply as some sort of Christian, evangelical crusade, we must also be careful not to give into the orientalizing simplification that Turkey is on this list simply because the tenets of Islam forbid alcohol. The reality is far more interesting. "Wherever the flag of a Christian nation has gone, there, under its folds and under its protection, has followed the hated liquor traffic," wrote the globe-trotting American prohibitionist Pussyfoot Johnson. "That is the situation that has stared me in the face in every Oriental country on earth dominated by a Christian power. That is the thing that the Moslem sees day by day."[42] So perhaps it is not surprising that in their push for independence from colonial domination nationalists like Mustafa Kemal Atatürk, in Turkey, would take aim at the debauching local effects of the colonial liquor traffic.

Administratively, the Ottoman Empire relied on a patchwork of autonomous confessional communities known as millets, which mediated between the individual and the state. Whether Muslim, Christian, or Jewish, these millets enforced public order, regulated legal and contractual disputes, and registered births, marriages, wills, and deaths. They also regulated alcohol: the Ottoman government required only a license and a tax paid on the manufacture of alcoholic beverages, and aside from during the fast of Ramadan, there were no penalties against alcohol consumption.[43]

Yet with defeat in World War I, the sultan's "capitulations" to European empires gave way to outright Allied occupation, with the occupiers breaking the former empire into "mandates" and "protectorates." Humiliated by the occupation and the inaction of the Istanbul government, field commander Mustafa Kemal rallied nationalist officers in Ankara, in the Anatolian heartland, where they established their own parliament, the Grand National Assembly (GNA). Waging a war of national liberation against the Allied and Greek forces, by 1923 Kemal's national army had pushed back the foreign occupiers—who took the last sultan with them—and by the Treaty of Lausanne gained full sovereignty over all Anatolia under a modern, secular Turkish republic.

One of the very first orders of business for Kemal's GNA in 1920 was the establishment of a national prohibition law. Yet the prohibition could only be implemented in the eastern and central areas, controlled by Kemal's forces in 1920. Their sovereignty extended to southwestern Turkey in 1921 with the withdrawal of the French, then to northwestern Turkey in 1922 with the expulsion of the Greeks, and finally to Istanbul and all of Turkey in 1923. Meanwhile, the British occupiers defied prohibition so long as they controlled the capital.[44] The Kemalist government sought to reinvent Turkey as a modern, secular republic with a thoroughly Westernized population. Consequently, debates over prohibition centered less on issues of morality and more on practical concerns over public health, state finance, and minimizing the influence of foreign nationals, who overwhelmingly profited from the Turkish liquor trade.[45]

Yet Turkish prohibition did not last long, giving way to a government monopolization scheme as early as 1924. Indeed, the final remnant of the system of Ottoman "capitulations" was the collection of excise to service the public debt, which had been outsourced to the Western powers. In its efforts to restore Turkish sovereignty, the nationalist government sought a way to pay off the remaining foreign debts. "There was a feeling that, inasmuch as the Christians drank most of the liquor and we wanted to get rid of them, it was best to inaugurate a temporary license law and let the Christians drink themselves to death while we made as much money as possible out of their undoing and [paid] the public debt."[46]

INDIA, 1939, 1947

No consideration of the global scope of prohibition would be complete without mention of Mahatma Gandhi's prohibitionism, which had roots similar to those of Atatürk's assertion of self-determination against colonial Britain. Gandhi professed that whether in India or South Africa or elsewhere, alcohol was an "enemy of mankind," a "curse of civilization," and "one of the most greatly-felt evils of the British rule."[47]

"Prohibition," Gandhi later wrote, "has been a passion ever since my close contact with the Indian immigrants in South Africa and also with the South Africans. I have seen with my own eyes the terrible scourge drink can be. It has ruined people morally, physically, economically and it has destroyed the sanctity and happiness of the home. My heart bleeds as I think of the disaster that comes in its wake and I have really pined for the immediate introduction of prohibition."[48] Accordingly, total abstinence was required of everyone living at Gandhi's South African communes.[49]

Once he was back in India, temperance and outright prohibition became the cornerstone of Gandhi's movement against British colonial domination. In some provinces, the British government manufactured the alcohol and farmed out the retail trade. Elsewhere, the colonial authorities auctioned off the rights both to distill liquors and to sell them. Aside from the land revenue, the excise on the liquor trade was the single largest source of government revenue (just as in imperial Russia and across Europe), constituting 31 percent of total revenues in the province of Madras and 33 percent in Bombay.[50] Since the financial power of the British Raj was built on alcohol, Gandhi's encouragement of both individual temperance and statutory prohibition constituted a grave threat to the status quo.

As with colonization elsewhere, temperance and the well-being of the population were sacrificed to maximizing revenue. By stigmatizing drinking as a foreign habit and a British imposition, India made abstinence synonymous with patriotism. Diminishing the liquor revenues collected by the colonial administration became a point of agreement between Hindus and Muslims, and along with the question of self-determination, became for nationalists another issue of moral superiority over their British overlords.[51] With such widespread subaltern support, in 1920 Gandhi led a movement of noncooperation against the Raj, employing nonviolence and peaceful resistance to authority. Among the tactics used was picketing taverns and liquor shops, admonishing those who frequented them to abstain. The tactic was surprisingly effective, with the auctions for the liquor-tax excise failing due to the movement.[52]

Still, the prohibition question became the touchstone of Gandhi's swaraj, or movement for nationalist liberation from British domination. Throughout the 1920s, 1930s, and 1940s, India was the main front of the global war on liquor, as at Gandhi's behest the Indian National Congress (INC) made prohibition the core of its independence platform. As Gandhi himself wrote, if he had the power, "the first thing I would do would be to close without compensation all the liquor shops, destroy all the toddy palms such as I know them in Gujarat, compel factory owners to produce humane conditions for their workmen and open refreshment and recreation rooms where these workmen would get innocent drinks and equally innocent amusements."[53]

Hoping to coopt the restive Indian independence movement, the 1935 Government of India Act devolved significant power over domestic politics—including the liquor trade—from the British Raj to the democratically elected INC. With their first taste of sovereignty, Gandhi's first charge to the new Congress ministries was to "enforce immediate prohibition by making [the Indian education budget] self-supporting instead of paying for it from the liquor revenue."[54] In 1939 the INC government stopped issuing liquor-selling licenses. As existing licenses lapsed and were not renewed, the effect was a gradual prohibition. The INC's policy was not to last: the British-controlled Bombay High Court annulled the prohibition in 1940, claiming that it was the British government's right to control the traffic between the Indian federal states.[55]

Ultimately, though, when the movement for Indian independence finally achieved India's liberation from the British in 1947, prohibition was written into India's constitution—though Prime Minister Jawaharlal Nehru left it to each federal state to determine to what degree it would be enforced. Even today, the 60 million inhabitants of Gujarat state are largely "dry," as are some regions of northeast India.[56]

CONCLUSION

Perhaps the most glaring commonality among these cases of alcohol prohibition is that they occurred nearly simultaneously as part of a global "prohibition wave" associated with the outbreak of World War I. In her contribution to this volume (chapter 4), Ann-Marie Szymanski argues that World War I was a proximate—rather than a primary—cause of American prohibition. This was just as true internationally as in the United States. In my study *The Political Power of Bad Ideas* (2010), I undertake a deeper, structural study of the policymaking process in multiple countries. In doing so, I find that the crisis of World War I acted as a catalyst, something akin to a reagent in a chemical reaction. Across the North Atlantic, the political and economic crises of war opened a window for dramatic policy change, for belligerents and bystanders alike. Politics as usual gave way to shortened time horizons. In the language of policy studies, issues of liquor control moved from the agenda-setting phase to policy decisions at breakneck speed. Policymakers moved from parallel information processing to serial processing, curtailing in-depth policy debate, shifting the locus of policymaking, and changing the focus of the discourse on alcohol use from issues of morality and the individual's liberty to imbibe to abstention as a necessary sacrifice for economic security and national defense. While such policy decisions were ultimately filtered through each country's individual legislative institutions, in the cases listed above these exigencies led to a preference for simple, prepackaged policy solutions, such as prohibition.[57]

In addition to helping us understand the catalyzing role of World War I, examining alcohol prohibition in comparative context can dispel many myths. Not only was prohibition not some manifestation of American exceptionalism but understanding the broader scope of prohibition calls into question the fundamental assumption that prohibition itself was some sort of "symbolic crusade" of midwestern evangelicals against the pressures of modernization and immigration. Internationally, prohibition was pursued not simply by Protestants but by Catholics, Orthodox Christians, Muslims, Hindus, and atheists as well. Moreover, the impulse toward prohibition—both around the world and in the United States—was less a moralizing "thou shalt not" imposed by Bible-thumping zealots than it was a movement against predatory big business and a colonial state in defense of democracy, self-determination, and community well-being.

NOTES

1. A. C. Archibald, "Explaining the World-Wide Prohibition Phenomena," *Union Signal*, 30 December 1915.

2. Mark Lawrence Schrad, "The Transnational Temperance Community and the Regulation of the Alcohol Traffic," in *Transnational Communities: Shaping Global Economic Governance*, ed. Marie-Laure Djelic and Sigrid Quack (Cambridge: Cambridge University Press, 2010).

3. Foreign Office, *Despatch from His Majesty's Minister at Brussels, Transmitting Convention Respecting Liquors in Africa*, Cd.3264 (London: Harrison & Sons, 1906), 2–5; Guy Hayler, *Prohibition Advance in All Lands; a Study of the World-Wide Character of the Drink Question*, 2nd ed. (London: International Prohibition Confederation, 1914), 203–8; John Newton, *Alcohol and Native Races: The Case of Our West African Colonies* (Westminster: The Native Races and the Liquor Traffic United Committee, 1915).

4. Mark Lawrence Schrad, "The First Social Policy: Alcohol Control and Modernity in Policy Studies," *Journal of Policy History* 19, no. 4 (2007): 437; Gallus Thomann, *Colonial Liquor Laws* (New York: United States Brewers' Association, 1887), 143–87.

5. Dawson Burns, *Temperance History: A Consecutive Narrative of the Rise, Development and Extension of the Temperance Reform*, 2 vols. (London: National Temperance Publication Depot, 1889), 1:120, 255.

6. Mark Lawrence Schrad, *Vodka Politics: Alcohol, Autocracy, and the Secret History of the Russian State* (New York: Oxford University Press, 2014), 124.

7. Vladimir N. Kokovtsov, *Out of My Past: The Memoirs of Count Kokovtsov*, trans. Laura Matveev (Stanford, CA: Stanford University Press, 1935), 444.

8. William Johnson, *The Liquor Problem in Russia* (Westerville, OH: American Issue Publishing House, 1915), 191.

9. George Snow, "Alcoholism in the Russian Military: The Public Sphere and the Temperance Discourse, 1883–1917," *Jahrbücher für Geschichte Osteuropas* 45, no. 3 (1997): 428–29.

10. See Schrad, *Vodka Politics*, 179–87.

11. *Russkoe slovo* (Moscow), 7 October 1914, excerpt reprinted in Johnson, *Liquor Problem in Russia*, 200. The same wording is found in the report of the tsar's council of ministers of the following day, 13 September (Old Style) /29 September (New Style): "No. 137. Osobyi zhurnal soveta ministrov. 13 sentyabrya 1914 goda: Ob usloviyakh svedeniya gosudarstvennoi rospisi dokhodov i raskhodov na 1915 god." *Osobye Zhurnaly Soveta Ministrov Rossiiskoi Imperii. 1909–1917 Gg. / 1914 God* [Special journals of the council of ministers of the Russian Empire, 1909–1917, for 1914] (Moscow: ROSSPEN, 2006), 364.

12. Mark Lawrence Schrad, "The Revolutionary Implications of Russian Alcohol Prohibition, 1914–1925," in *Russia's Great War and Revolution, 1914–22: The Centennial Reappraisal*, ed. Christopher Read, Peter Waldron, and Adele Lindenmeyr (Bloomington, IN: Slavica, 2018), 45–63.

13. D. N. Voronov, *O samogone* (Moscow, 1929), 6, quoted in *Under the Influence: Working-Class Drinking, Temperance, and Cultural Revolution in Russia, 1895–1932*, by Kate Transchel (Pittsburgh: University of Pittsburgh Press, 2006), 70; Schrad, *Vodka Politics*, 190.

14. Schrad, "Revolutionary Implications of Russian Alcohol Prohibition," 60.

15. State Archives of the Russian Federation (GARF), f. 579 (Milyukov, Pavel Nikolaevich), op. 1, d. 2547 (Tezisy k dokladu A. I. Shingareva "Voina, trezvost' i finansy" [Abstracts to A. I. Shingareva's report "War, Sobriety and Finance"]),1.1. For an English translation, see Michael T. Florinsky, *The End of the Russian Empire* (New York: Collier Books, 1961), 44.

16. W. Arthur McKee, "Sukhoi zakon v gody Pervoi Mirovoi Voiny: Prichiny, kontseptsiya i posledstviya vvedeniya sukhogo zakona v Rossii: 1914–1917 gg." [Dry laws in the year of the First World War: Causes, conceptions and consequences of the introduction of dry laws in Russia: 1914–1917], in *Rossiya i pervaya mirovaya voina (Materialy mezhdunarodnogo nauchnogo kollokviuma)* [Russia in the First World War (Materals of the International Scholarly Colloquium)] (St. Petersburg: Izdatel'stvo "Dmitrii Bulanin," 1999), 149; M. Bogolepoff, "Public Finance," in *Russia: Its Trade and Commerce*, ed. Arthur Raffalovich (London: P. S. King & Son, 1918), 346.

17. Quoted in Kokovtsov, *Out of My Past*, 473.

18. Aleksandr P. Pogrebinskii, *Ocherki istorii finanasov dorevolyutsionnoi Rossii (XIX–XX vv.)* [Essays on the history of finance in prerevolutionary Russia (19th and 20th centuries)] (Moscow: Gosfinizdat, 1954), 126–28.

19. *Pravda*, 15 March 1913; Vladimir I. Lenin, "Spare Cash," in *Collected Works Volume 18: April 1912–March 1913* (Moscow: Progress Publishers, 1963).

20. "Bei, no ne do smerti," *Zarya*, April 1901; Vladimir I. Lenin, "Beat—but Not to Death!," in *Collected Works Volume 4: 1898–April 1901* (Moscow: Progress Publishers, 1960).

21. Schrad, *Vodka Politics*, 202–3.

22. E. Shirvindt, F. Traskovich, and M. Gernet, eds., *Problemy prestupnosti: Sbornik* [Problems of crime: A collection], vol. 4 (Moscow: Izdatel'stvo narodnogo komissariata vnutrennikh del RSFSR, 1929), 116.

23. Vladimir I. Lenin, "X vserossiiskaya konferentsiya RKP(b)" [Tenth all-Russian conference of the Russian Communist Party (Bolsheviks], in *Sochineniya, tom 32: Dekabr' 1920–avgust 1921* [Collected works, volume 32: December 1920–August 1921] (Moscow: Gosudarstvennoe izdatel'stvo politicheskoi literatury, 1951), 403.

24. Joseph Stalin, "Pis'mo Shinkevichu (20 Marta 1927 g.)" [Letter to Shinkevich, 20 March 1937], in *Sochineniya, tom 9: Dekabr' 1926-iyul' 1927* [Collected Works, volume 9: December 1926–July 1927] (Moscow: Gosudarstvennoe izdatel'stvo politicheskoi literatury, 1948), 191.

25. Frank Eckelt, "The Rise and Fall of the Béla Kun Regime in 1919" (PhD diss., New York University, 1966), 221.

26. John Wuorinen, "Finland's Prohibition Experiment," *Annals of the American Academy of Political and Social Science* 163 (1932): 217.

27. "Finland," in *Standard Encyclopedia of the Alcohol Problem*, ed. Ernest H. Cherrington, 6 vols. (Westerville, OH: American Issue Publishing House, 1925–30), 3:991.

28. Wuorinen, "Finland's Prohibition Experiment," 218.

29. Wuorinen, "Finland's Prohibition Experiment," 222; John Wuorinen, *The Prohibition Experiment in Finland* (New York: Columbia University Press, 1931).

30. "Esthonia," in Cherrington, *Standard Encyclopedia of the Alcohol Problem*, 3:950–52.

31. "Belgium," in Cherrington, *Standard Encyclopedia of the Alcohol Problem*, 1:315.

32. Rod Phillips, *Alcohol: A History* (Chapel Hill: University of North Carolina Press, 2014), 277; Emile Vandervelde, *The Attitude of the Socialist Party toward the Alcohol Question: A Paper Read at the Tenth International Congress against Alcoholism* (Westerville, OH: American Issue Publishing Company, 1907), 12, 16.

33. Hildigunnur Ólafsdóttir, "The Entrance of Beer into a Persistent Spirits Culture," *Contemporary Drug Problems* 26 (1999).

34. Helgi Gunnlaugsson, "Iceland's Peculiar Beer Ban, 1915–1989," in *Dual Markets: Comparative Approaches to Regulation*, ed. Ernesto U. Savona, Mark A. R. Kleiman, and Francesco Calderoni (New York: Springer, 2017), 237–43.

35. "Norway," in Cherrington, *Standard Encyclopedia of the Alcohol Problem*, 5:2027.

36. Statistisk sentralbyrå [Norwegian statistical bureau], accessed 11 July 2018, http://www.ssb.no/histstat/aarbok/ht-000130-004.html. See also Tor Bjørklund, *Hundre år med folkeavstemninger Norge og norden 1905–2005* [One hundred years of referendums in Norway and the Nordic region, 1905–2005] (Oslo: Universitetsforlaget, 2005).

37. Association Against the Prohibition Amendment, *Norway's Noble Experiment* (Washington, DC: AAPA, 1931); "Norway," 2031.

38. Association Against the Prohibition Amendment, *Government Liquor Control in Canada* (Washington, DC: AAPA, 1930).

39. Reginald G. Smart and Alan C. Ogborne, *Northern Spirits: A Social History of Alcohol in Canada*, 2nd ed. (Toronto: Ontario Addiction Research Foundation, 1996), 44.

40. "Canada," in Cherrington, *Standard Encyclopedia of the Alcohol Problem*, 2:500.

41. "Newfoundland and Labrador," in Cherrington, *Standard Encyclopedia of the Alcohol Problem*, 4:1903.

42. William E. Johnson, "Babylon and Way Stations" (1930), chap. 3, pp. 7–8, MS at New York State Historical Society, Cooperstown, NY.

43. Charles King, *Midnight at the Pera Palace: The Birth of Modern Istanbul* (New York: Norton, 2014), 143; "Turkey," in Cherrington, *Standard Encyclopedia of the Alcohol Problem*, 6:2683–87.

44. "Turkey," 2685.

45. Emine Ö. Evered and Kyle T. Evered, "A Geopolitics of Drinking: Debating the Place of Alcohol in Early Republican Turkey," *Political Geography* 50 (2016): 54–56; Canan Balkan, "The Anti-Alcohol Movement in the Early Republican Period in Turkey" (abstract of MA thesis, Bogaziçi University, 2012).

46. Quoted in "Turkey," i2685–86.

47. Ramachandra Guha, *Gandhi before India* (New York: Random House, 2014), 48.

48. Mohandas K. Gandhi, "Interview to Deputation of Victuallers' Association. June 2, 1939," in *The Collected Works of Mahatma Gandhi* (New Delhi: Publications Division, Government of India, 1939), 8, available online at http://www.gandhiashramsevagram.org/gandhi-literature/collected-works-of-mahatma-gandhi-volume-1-to-98.php, accessed 23 June 2016.

49. David Fahey and Padma Manian, "Poverty and Purification: The Politics of Gandhi's Campaign for Prohibition," *Historian* 67, no. 3 (2005): 494.

50. Fahey and Manian, "Poverty and Purification," 498; Colonial Office, *Reply to Representations and Statements Submitted by Mr. Herbert Roberts, M.P., Relative to Excise Administration in India*, Cd.4488 (London: Darling & Son, 1909), 3, 13–15.

51. Fahey and Manian, "Poverty and Purification," 490–91; Carolyn Heitmeyer and Edward Simpson, "The Culture of Prohibition in Gujarat, India," in *A History of Alcohol and Drugs in Modern South Asia: Intoxicating Affairs*, ed. Harald Fischer-Tiné and Jana Tschurenev (New York: Routledge, 2014), 210.

52. Robert Eric Colvard, "A World without Drink: Temperance in Modern India, 1880–1940" (PhD diss., University of Iowa, 2013), 180.

53. Quoted in Fahey and Manian, "Poverty and Purification," 500.

54. Ramachandra Guha, *Gandhi: The Years That Changed the World, 1914–1948* (New York: Knopf, 2018), 506, 513–14.

55. *Sheth Chinubhai Lalbhai et al. v. Emperor,* Bombay High Court, 11 April 1940, accessed 8 November 2018, https://www.casemine.com/judgement/in/56b49357607d ba348f0066e6.

56. Heitmeyer and Simpson, "Culture of Prohibition in Gujarat," 210.

57. Mark Lawrence Schrad, *The Political Power of Bad Ideas: Networks, Institutions, and the Global Prohibition Wave* (New York: Oxford University Press, 2010), 10–11, 203.

MYTH 9

PROHIBITION CHANGED LITTLE ABOUT AMERICAN DRINKING HABITS

GARRETT PECK

A local blog featured a story about a well-known chef launching a lawsuit against Virginia regulations that forbade him from advertising happy hour. In the comments section, I explained how states such as Virginia set up awkward alcohol regulations in the wake of prohibition that often don't reflect our current values—and in this case might even impede our freedom of speech. "Cultural norms around temperance and the movement's political influence have fallen by the wayside," I wrote. A commentator countered my statement: "The majority of American citizens in 1934 thought prohibition was not good public policy. Likewise, it is not accurate to state that 'cultural norms' at the time are much different than today. The prohibition movement was a loud, active, and influential body, but it hardly represented the majority."[1]

How I begged to differ. Everything about American drinking habits has changed in the decades since prohibition ended. Our drinking habits continue to evolve, as drinking is part of our evolving culture. Prohibition left the United States with maladjusted social attitudes toward alcohol that took decades to heal; in fact, we still have not gotten over the

"Noble Experiment." As I wrote in my first book, *The Prohibition Hangover,* "The social stigma against drinking has worn off, yet everywhere we hear the legacy of Prohibition, echoing down the years long after the temperance bell stopped ringing."[2]

PROHIBITION AND REPEAL

Much of the American public took a quiet, wait-and-see attitude when national prohibition began on January 16, 1920. But as the decade progressed and organized crime took over cities, inciting corruption and violence, the public turned deeply cynical. Bootleggers were everywhere, and though booze was expensive, people were still drinking in countless speakeasies. Americans had become a nation of scofflaws, and even Congress was employing bootleggers.

All prohibition effectively did was to deregulate the alcohol market; the consumer had no idea what he or she was buying. The genuine Scotch the bootlegger offered was more likely industrial alcohol with a bit of caramel food coloring and turpentine for that peaty, fresh-from-the-Highlands smell. Likewise for "bathtub gin." *Caveat emptor* ruled.

The stock market crash of 1929 and the subsequent Great Depression signaled the death knell of prohibition as opponents realized that legalizing booze could create jobs and generate tax revenue. The midterm congressional election of 1930 was a wet wave. Voters rejected the ostensibly dry Republicans and replaced them with openly wet Democrats, who were loudly calling for an end to prohibition. Just two years later, the nation elected to the presidency Franklin Delano Roosevelt, who ran on the repeal platform.

FDR fulfilled a campaign promise to legalize beer early in his administration. Congress simply mandated that 3.2 percent beer was not intoxicating and thus did not violate the Eighteenth Amendment or the Volstead Act, which enforced it. Roosevelt signed the bill into law, and at midnight on April 7, 1933, the United States staged its first big repeal party. Much of the country took to the streets and celebrated with pints of beer that cost just a nickel. The Yuengling Brewery, of Pennsylvania, dropped off the first two cases of legal beer at the White House for President Roosevelt. In the early morning hours of "New Beers Eve," Americans knew prohibition would soon be history.[3] And it soon was. States lined up to ratify the Twenty-First Amendment, repealing prohibition. Michigan was first, voting just three days after New Beers Eve. The votes took place at a blistering pace, putting the amendment over the top in just eight months. On December 5, Utah became the thirty-sixth state to ratify the amendment, driving the final nail in the prohibition coffin. The date is forever known as Repeal Day, but in more recent years it has been referred to as Cinco de Drinko. The "Thirteen Awful Years," as literary critic H. L. Mencken called them, were over.[4]

Prohibition intended to stop American drinking, but Demon Rum refused to die. Now that alcohol was legal again, how to stuff the genie back into the bottle? How to get this beast back under control? Leadership came from a surprising direction: John D. Rockefeller Jr., a dry Baptist who was the wealthiest man in the country. He was a former prohibition supporter who publicly broke with the dry movement in a widely circulated New York Times op-ed in 1932. Rockefeller sponsored a commission that looked at how to regulate alcohol after prohibition. The commission published its findings in a landmark 1933 book called Towards Liquor Control, and these regulatory suggestions were largely adopted as states established the three-tier system.[5]

The three-tier system was designed to break apart the vertical integration of the alcohol industry that had existed before prohibition. No longer could breweries distribute beer or own bars. The tiers were now the alcohol producer, such as a brewery, distillery, or winery; the distributor or wholesaler; and the retailer, whether a bar, a liquor store, or a supermarket. Thirty-two states adopted this License model, while the other eighteen became Control States. In this latter model, the state itself distributes and sells alcohol, such as one sees at state-owned package stores in New Hampshire, Pennsylvania, and Utah. To further complicate things, some Control States, such as Virginia, allow beer and wine to be privately sold at supermarkets, while distilled spirits are sold at state-run liquor stores. As the wine industry developed, many Control States would come to allow wineries to sell their products directly to customers.

Many of the country's alcohol regulations date from 1934, in the immediate wake of repeal. The Twenty-First Amendment gave states the power to regulate alcohol within their borders, and each state had to establish an alcohol beverage control (ABC) regulatory regime. Some states were more lenient than others, but they all sought to clamp down on the environment in which people could purchase and consume alcohol. For example, many states banned bars from allowing customers to stand or walk around while holding a drink. If a customer wanted to move to another table, a porter had to carry the customer's drink. This was in part to increase employment during the Great Depression. Most states banned Sunday alcohol sales in a nod to Sabbatarians. Consumers chafed at these restrictions.

Many Americans today, knowing that people still drink, might conclude that prohibition altered nothing. Yet much has evolved since that first Repeal Day in 1933. There have been many changes in what Americans drink, where they drink, how much they consume, and how they feel about people who drink.

HOW DID PROHIBITION CHANGE AMERICAN DRINKING?

Toward the end of prohibition, the wet crusader and propagandist Rufus Lusk noted how prohibition had fundamentally altered the country's drinking habits: "The drinking of hard liquor has increased until the country has lost its taste for good beer and wines."[6] Before prohibition, Americans overwhelmingly drank lager beer, under the influence (so to speak) of the wave of Germans who arrived beginning in the 1840s, but during prohibition beer became scarce. Bootleggers brought to market bathtub gin, often renatured industrial alcohol with flavorings, as it was highly concentrated alcohol and therefore more profitable than beer or wine. (One sees parallels in the modern Drug Wars, where marijuana has evolved into higher concentrations of THC, where cocaine has evolved into crack, and where opioids have evolved into the highly addictive and sometimes deadly fentanyl.) To mask the nastiness of the booze, drinkers often resorted to sweet additives like ginger ale or soda pop to make cocktails palatable. Prohibition pushed Americans away from beer and toward distilled spirits.

Christian Heurich, the largest brewer in Washington, DC, successfully opened his brewery after prohibition but quickly noted how much of the beer market had evaporated. "We made every effort not to have a shortage of beer, but soon we discovered that the public had forgotten about drinking beer!" He added, "Our sales increased slowly, but they were nothing in comparison to our sales before prohibition."[7]

Brewers everywhere were confronted by the same truth. To make matters worse, people lacked the money for beer during the Great Depression. With a quarter of the American workforce unemployed, too few people could splurge on a drink. The drinking culture had shifted away from saloons and toward home consumption. Desperate to capitalize on the home market, the Krueger Brewing Company, in Richmond, Virginia, invented the beer can in 1935.

Temperance leaders swore they would be back and that prohibition was not over. But it was. The generation of temperance leaders gradually died off. Wayne Wheeler, the legislative superintendent for the Anti-Saloon League and the person most responsible for the Eighteenth Amendment, died in 1927. The former baseball star and temperance tent–revivalist preacher Billy Sunday met his maker in 1935. The Woman's Christian Temperance Union's Ella Boole passed away in 1953. Temperance died with them, and the word faded from America's cultural vocabulary, such that most people today can't even define what the temperance movement stood for: abstinence from alcohol. They know about prohibition and often romanticize it, but they cannot explain why it happened.

Even so, the alcoholic beverage industry remained concerned for decades that prohibitionists would resurrect the movement. Distilled spirits especially were distrusted, which is why distillers' trade associations voluntarily banned radio and television advertising into the 1990s. The brewing industry had no such restraints, which gave beer a big edge.

The generation that fought World War II, often called the Greatest Generation, grew up during prohibition and saw how the Noble Experiment failed to stop people from drinking. They chose to drink, and beer became part of GI rations during the war. Both men and women drank heavily during and after the war. This generation did not embrace the culture war over alcohol but moved on to other battles—over civil rights, communism, and fascism.

WHAT ARE AMERICANS DRINKING?

Just how normalized has alcohol consumption become since repeal in 1933? Almost every year since 1939, Gallup has surveyed Americans about their drinking habits. Although the number varies from year to year, the survey has consistently shown that two-thirds of Americans drink alcoholic beverages. Men prefer beer (in part because beer has long been marketed to men), while women prefer wine. Both sexes drink distilled spirits. Beer remains our national alcoholic beverage, but it had to claw its way back to the top after prohibition.[8]

Beer emerged deeply wounded from prohibition. Some 756 breweries managed to reopen in 1934, but with too little market demand many of them closed. Some of them produced bad beer, further undermining the market. Within two decades their numbers were cut in half. By 1978 there were only 89 breweries in the United States, and the surviving national brewers—dominated by Anheuser-Busch, Pabst, and Schlitz—focused on fizzy, lightweight, mass-produced beer that was simply a commodity. Beer was dumbed down as the brewers engaged in a trade war over light lager.[9]

Once President Jimmy Carter legalized home brewing in 1978, the nascent craft-brewing industry began to rise. This first wave lasted through the 1990s and then experienced a sharp downturn, during which many "microbrewers" (as they were then called) went out of business, as they lacked sufficient business plans. A second wave of craft brewing began around the time of the Great Recession (2007–8), when American consumers shifted toward cheaper luxuries. Good beer was less expensive than wine by the glass at a restaurant. Brewers seized the moment, quitting their day jobs to open thousands of brewpubs and craft breweries around the country at breathtaking speed. According to the Brewers Association, there were 6,372 breweries operating in the United States in 2017. Beer remains the most popular alcoholic beverage among Americans, though it has come under threat in recent years from distilled spirits, which are capturing market share.[10]

Rum was popular during the colonial era, then subsumed by whiskey, only to rocket back to popularity during World War II as bourbon distilleries were converted to produce solvents, leaving Caribbean rum manufacturers to satisfy the American thirst for booze. The Trader Vic's restaurant chain, founded in Oakland, California, introduced Tiki to the country, a fad that raged during the 1950s. Tiki isn't an actual place but rather an American fantasy, combining Polynesian culture from the Pacific with Caribbean rum cocktails like the Fog Cutter and the Mai Tai in fanciful, Easter Island–like mugs.

Bourbon became especially popular among the Greatest Generation, but their children, the eternally young Baby Boomers, rejected anything with the word *old* in its name (Old Forester, Old Granddad, etc.). The bourbon industry nearly collapsed in the 1970s, leaving the Kentucky countryside littered with abandoned distillery complexes. The whiskey industry finally began to recover in the first decade of the twenty-first century as younger generations rediscovered aged brown spirits.

The migration of Americans to the Sunbelt led to a rising preference for cold mixed drinks based on white spirits like gin, light rum, tequila, and especially vodka. Despite the Cold War, traditional Russian vodka became the spirit of choice and has reigned supreme for decades; colorless and odorless, it can be slipped into almost any cocktail and still get the job done. The Moscow Mule combined vodka with ginger beer and required a special copper mug. The colorful and fruity Cosmopolitan was flavorful, but as people adopted the latest diet fad and fled in terror from calories and carbohydrates, some adopted the ultrabland vodka and soda as their fix (I shudder even typing this sentence). Today's cocktail culture takes its cues from the kitchen, offering fresh and unique ingredients mixed by bartenders who have made a career out of inventiveness.

Prohibition eviscerated the wine industry, and a national wine market did not reemerge until the 1960s. During the Noble Experiment, people could make homemade wine with raisin bricks, shifting American palates toward sweet wines. Likewise, bootleggers sold rotgut liquor often masked with soda pop or ginger ale, again shifting the palate toward sweetness. Prohibition did nothing to assuage the American sweet tooth and subsequent health issues like diabetes and obesity.

Wine-producing states such as California and New York made high-quality wine before prohibition, but little was exported out of state. During prohibition, much of the quality grape stock was ripped out and replaced by orchards of sweet table grapes that were turned into raisins. It took decades for the wine industry to recover. In the 1960s, winemaking pioneers in California's Napa Valley began experimenting with higher-quality varietals, and American wine began its inexorable rise in quality that would eventually challenge European wineries in the 1970s. Tourism fostered the wine industry's recovery. It didn't hurt that Napa and neighboring Sonoma County were stunningly picturesque. Wineries began opening tasting rooms, which brought in tourists, who would leave with their car trunks full of bottles of wine to be opened at dinner parties, as Americans likewise embraced gourmet food. Brewers and distillers would eventually catch on to the fact that tourism generated lifelong and devoted customers. Temperance-minded states shifted their stance once they realized how many jobs were being created and that alcohol production drives economic development.

Over time, consumers rebelled against restrictions on their freedom to drink. Today happy hour is an occasion to network with a business card or résumé in one hand and a beverage in the other. Alcohol producers likewise challenged the three-tier system and knocked many loopholes in it. In most states, breweries and brewpubs sell pints of beer and fill growlers; distillers offer tastings and sell bottles directly to visitors, even in dry counties; and wineries ship direct to consumers across state borders, the subject of a landmark US Supreme Court case in 2005, *Granholm v. Heald.*

WHERE DO AMERICANS DRINK?

The temperance movement targeted the saloon and the speakeasy as sources of all social evil, but bars emerged from prohibition intact, though they have had to continually adapt to changing consumer habits and tastes. It is certainly cheaper to imbibe at home, but then one misses the communality and conversation from sharing drinks with friends. People are ultimately social creatures, so we continue to frequent bars. In addition, brewpubs, distilleries, and wineries have opened up tasting rooms, allowing people to consume drinks at the site where the beverages were born.

In more recent years, the internet and smartphones have provided a new challenge to bars. Dating and hookup apps give people a reason to skip bars to meet their potential significant others, future exes, or sex partners; however, people continue visiting bars to watch sports, try fancy cocktails, eat dinner, play Monday night trivia, and meet up with friends. A gay bar owner once told me that he would never open a gay bar in the twenty-first century: today's young adults just want to be where their friends are, whether gay or straight. The bar has become far more integrated. Keep in mind that before prohibition, women were explicitly excluded from entering bars.

HOW MUCH ALCOHOL DO AMERICANS CONSUME?

William Rorabaugh, the godfather of American drinking history, estimated in his seminal 1979 book *The Alcoholic Republic* how much Americans have drunk since colonial days. Drinking peaked in 1830 at 3.9

gallons of ethanol annually (and at an astonishing 7.1 gallons when limited to just men of drinking age), a consumption rate that helped spawn the temperance movement. In 1915, the last time alcohol consumption was measured before national prohibition began, Americans drank only 1.6 gallons per person annually, as state dry laws limited availability.[11]

American drinking roared back in the wake of prohibition, but with nothing like the consumption rates seen in the 1830s. Twentieth-century consumption peaked at 2.76 gallons of ethanol per person annually in 1981, then steadily declined to 2.24 gallons in 2005. In the recovery from the Great Recession of 2007–8, American consumption increased slightly to 2.32 gallons annually in 2014. Federal guidelines recommend that no one drink more than 2.1 gallons of ethanol annually and that men limit themselves to two drinks per day, while women should consume no more than one drink per day. Five drinks at a single sitting is considered binge drinking by federal standards.[12]

HOW DO WE FEEL ABOUT PEOPLE WHO DRINK?

One noticeable change that occurred after prohibition was a better understanding of addiction. The temperance movement considered drinking to be sinful. It widely denounced drunkards and drunkenness, backed by the leading pseudoscience of the day—like pouring alcohol on a sheep's brain to scare children into not drinking, just as a later anti-drug television commercial would use a frying pan and eggs with the slogan "This is your brain. And this is your brain on drugs." Scientists such as E. M. Jellinek began studying addiction in the 1940s and classified alcoholism as a disease. Jellinek established the Yale Center for Alcohol Studies, which he later moved to Rutgers University as the Center of Alcohol Studies.

Two men desperate for sobriety, William Wilson (Bill W.) and Dr. Robert Smith (Dr. Bob), founded Alcoholics Anonymous in 1935, providing a community-based self-help organization for alcoholics. Four years later they published the book *Alcoholics Anonymous,* known to many as "The Big Book." AA has proven more effective and more lasting than earlier self-help organizations such as the Washingtonians in the 1850s, which simply required members to pledge not to drink, a promise that was too easy to break. AA acknowledges that individual recovery is almost hopeless without the help of a community and a spiritual higher power, whatever that higher power is to the person. Those who refrain from drinking are referred to as being in "recovery."

American cultural norms around alcohol changed significantly in the decades after repeal. Drinking alcohol in public once carried a heavy stigma, particularly among Protestants, that lingered for years. That gradually fell by the wayside, as did blue laws that banned Sunday alcohol sales and the shrinking number of dry counties. More Americans now embrace alcohol as a normal part of their lives, and many people see it as a healthy addition (in moderation) that improves their cardiovascular health. Alcohol certainly isn't medicine, but people in late middle age with rising cholesterol today are sometimes advised by their doctors to drink a glass of red wine a day.

The public-health community, meanwhile, views alcohol solely as a risk with no upside. The World Health Organization concluded that there is no safe level of alcohol consumption. A report in the *Lancet* in early 2018 showed that many early studies of healthy drinkers left out unhealthy people who formerly drank, which skewed the results. That same publication published a major study later that year focusing on rising risks in twenty-three alcohol-related areas. It looked at populations rather than individuals. The authors concluded that there is a low increase in risk to the individual for moderate drinking, but risk certainly skyrockets with heavy drinking. Even with these new studies, one should not expect to see much change in American drinking habits. Alcohol is too culturally ingrained, and the uncertain long-term health consequences from drinking are outweighed by the immediate joy of a beer after work. It is impossible to live a risk-free life. The physician father of one of my friends is fond of saying, "If you live healthy, you'll still die healthy," and he encourages people to live a little.[13]

Changes in American drinking patterns certainly aren't all positive or even neutral. One of the larger risks associated with alcohol is drunk driving. When prohibition became law, automobiles were just starting to see widespread adoption, and though people knew that driving after drinking was dangerous, they did it anyway. Today we are far more aware of the dangers, and yet driving under the influence still occurs, despite the widespread prevalence of cabs, designated drivers, and rideshare apps on smartphones.

Mothers Against Drunk Driving, or MADD, formed in 1980 and successfully lobbied to raise the drinking age in the United States from eighteen to twenty-one. This in turn has turned alcohol into a taboo that teenagers eagerly embrace, as alcohol is easy to get (it is often in the home already, or a friend or older sibling can buy it for them). Americans do a poor job of teaching young adults how to drink responsibly, and yet we are somehow surprised when teenagers and young adults binge drink. For them, drinking is about getting drunk, not about enhancing a meal or stimulating conversation.[14]

Americans have concluded that we are indeed a drinking nation, and we are now no longer shy or apologetic about that fact. Most of us are social drinkers, and many of us worship at the altar of high-quality alcoholic beverages. Since the turn of the twenty-first century, Americans have embraced all drinks handmade with the resurrection of craft beer, craft cocktails, and family wineries. This is a tradition that started in 1607 at Jamestown, where the settlers hoped to produce wine (they settled on tobacco instead), and it continues to this day. American drinking habits have evolved significantly since prohibition, even if we no longer view drinking as a sin.

NOTES

1. Bridget Reed Morawski, "Arlington Bar Owners Cheer Chef Geoff's Happy Hour Lawsuit," 29 March 2018, https://www.arlnow.com.

2. Garrett Peck, *The Prohibition Hangover: Alcohol in America from Demon Rum to Cult Cabernet* (New Brunswick, NJ: Rutgers University Press, 2009), 7.

3. "Many Cities Celebrate," *New York Times,* 7 April 1933; "Roosevelt Gets First Case of Capital's 3.2 Beer," *New York Times,* 7 April 1933.

4. H. L. Mencken, *My Life as Author and Editor* (New York: Knopf, 1993), 257; Mencken, *Heathen Days, 1890–1936* (Baltimore: Johns Hopkins University Press, 1996), 206.

5. "Text of Rockefeller's Letter to Dr. Butler," *New York Times,* 7 June 1932.

6. Rufus S. Lusk, "The Drinking Habit," *Annals of the American Academy of Political and Social Science* 163 (September 1932): 52.

7. Christian Heurich, *From My Life: 1842–1934,* transcribed and ed. Eda Offutt (Washington, DC: privately published, 1934).

8. "Beer Remains the Preferred Alcoholic Beverage in the U.S.," 19 July 2017, https://news.gallup.com/poll/214229.

9. "Number of Breweries: Historical U.S. Brewery Count, Brewers Association," https://www.brewersassociation.org/statistics/numberofbreweries/.

10. "Number of Breweries: Historical U.S. Brewery Count, Brewers Association."

11. William J. Rorabaugh, *The Alcoholic Republic: An American Tradition* (New York: Oxford University Press, 1979), 232–33.

12. Sarah P. Haughwout, Robin A. LaVallee, and I-Jen P. Castle, "Apparent Per Capital Alcohol Consumption: National, State, and Regional Trends, 1977–2014," March 2016, Surveillance Report #104, National Institute of Alcohol Abuse and Alcoholism, https://pubs.niaaa.nih.gov/publications/surveillance104/CONS14.htm.

13. Joel Achenbach, "Safest Level of Consumption is None, Worldwide Study Shows," *Washington Post,* 23 August 2018.

14. For Mothers Against Drunk Driving, see www.madd.org.

MYTH 10

THE CURRENT DEBATES OVER MARIJUANA LEGALIZATION ARE THE SAME AS THOSE THAT ENDED PROHIBITION

BOB L. BEACH

I grew up during the "Just Say No" campaigns of the Reagan administration. One of my most memorable anti-drug school assemblies in junior high was a lecture on the dangers of drugs based on the speaker's own experience with drug abuse and addiction. The horrifying conclusion to his relatively somber spoken remarks was a video montage that could only be described as an R-rated version of the eighties cult VHS series *Faces of Death*. Weeks of nightmares following that assembly notwithstanding, I developed a guilty fascination with drugs and drug use and came to appreciate the efforts of education and law-enforcement officials to scare us straight. I was proud that I had made it through high school without touching any intoxicating substances, including alcohol.

College experimentation with both alcohol and marijuana redirected my fascination, as the violent films in junior high and subsequent "education" in high school and early college from our elders about the dangers of both substances seemed to have been based less on their actual effects and more on a misguided attempt by adults in positions of authority to maintain control over their children. From that generational rage, the growing popular culture around marijuana, and the "history" of the drug's prohibition shared among friends during intense smoking sessions, I concluded that marijuana prohibition in the United States was at best arbitrary and at worst a serious miscarriage of justice.

Meanwhile, public attitudes toward the drug were beginning to change, and people began to publicly question the logic of the drug war, especially the war on marijuana. My secretive subgroup's views were coming more into line with the mainstream. In 1996, California voters approved Proposition 215, an initiative that gave patients access to medical marijuana. Activist groups hailed the decision as the first major "pullback" in the war on drugs since the repeal of alcohol in 1933.[1] Public support for medical and even recreational marijuana use made its gradual but inexorable climb through the first decade of this century and continues today, and further comparisons between a "new repeal" moment and the prohibition moment have become difficult to ignore.

Armed with this increasingly popular belief that marijuana prohibition was destined to fail as the Eighteenth Amendment had, I was introduced to the idea that my childhood fascination with drugs could become a serious career option at the very end of my master's program at Rutgers University in 2009. Three years later, as I began my doctoral program as a drug historian, Colorado and Washington became the first states to legalize recreational marijuana sales. By 2018, ten states and Washington, DC, had legalized some form of recreational marijuana, and thirty-nine states in total have some form of marijuana legalization, for medical reasons. According to the *Business Insider,* a full 64 percent of Americans now favor full legalization, and legal sales almost topped $10 billion in 2017.[2] It seems that decisive action to remove restrictions on marijuana at the federal level is only a matter of time.

As I began to learn more about the history of marijuana, the simple comparison to alcohol became more difficult to maintain. Unlike prohibition, which only lasted thirteen years, the restriction of marijuana continues at the federal level more than a century after the first restrictive laws were passed, eighty years after the first explicit ban at the federal level, and almost a quarter century since the "first" cracks appeared in support for the war on drugs in California. Despite the optimistic enthusiasm for the "history repeats itself" comparisons to the Twenty-First Amendment on the part of pro-marijuana activists, the halting progress of marijuana legalization is a testament to the power and influence of the supporters of the war on drugs. The election of Donald Trump adds to the growing dread among activists that we are ready to take a significant step backward, yet again. And indeed, there is still a long way to go.

In considering historical comparisons between alcohol and marijuana in this essay, I will argue that despite some interesting but largely superficial similarities between the two historical moments, the differences are the result of the unique historical trajectories of the two substances in the American experience. These similarities, though striking, can be explained through marijuana's role, subservient to alcohol and other drugs, in larger social concerns about drug abuse, addiction, and their related social and economic effects. Providing the lone marijuana perspective in this book, this essay constitutes a comparison of the two movements, but the comparison will weave its way through a discussion of marijuana's historical trajectory in the United States.

While a full accounting of the differences would constitute its own volume, my comparison here examines the long introduction of the plant *cannabis sativa* to the United States, the multi-dimensional roots of the 1937 Marijuana Tax Act (MTA), and the tensions between supporters of suppression and supporters of tolerance in the period after the MTA. We will see that unlike the story of alcohol prohibition and repeal, which was heavily influenced by the intractable role of alcohol in society, the story of the longer-running new prohibition and repeal highlights a reluctance to fully accept the use of marijuana in American society.

CONFRONTING THE MYTH

In 2014, eighteen years after passage of Prop 215 and in the context of a rising wave of public support for legalization, the *New York Times* editorial board was urging lawmakers to "Repeal Prohibition, Again." By then, comparisons to prohibition's repeal were becoming commonplace as the public support for relaxing marijuana restrictions reached new highs. In the introductory piece to a series of *Times* articles on the legalization debate, the editors contrasted the speed with which the United States "[came] to its senses" on prohibition with the "foot dragging" on legalizing marijuana.[3] A nonscientific sampling of editorials from other papers around the country during this time reveals a similar spike in public pronouncements in favor of reform, most emphasizing the "eerie," "intriguing," "uncanny," and even "identical" similarities between the two movements.[4]

To be sure, there are indeed several familiar refrains reminiscent of the debates over alcohol within those about marijuana legalization today. Most of these comparisons involve the problems associated with the enforcement of prohibition, including the increase in political and economic corruption, the general disrespect for laws, and the rise of organized crime in the manufacture and distribution of the illicit product, motivated by profits and operating with unacceptable levels of violence. Others highlight unique or trailblazing roles played by states like Colorado, California, and Massachusetts during both debate periods, illustrating the long-running conflicts between local and federal priorities. As popular support for legalizing marijuana approached a tipping point around the onset of the Great Recession, the election of Barack Obama in 2008 elicited clearer and more frequent comparisons in popular discourse between marijuana legalization and the repeal plank on the 1932 Democratic Party platform. All this despite the candidate's and the party's avoidance of the issue in 2008 and Obama's permissive but largely lukewarm support for relaxation of marijuana laws as president.[5]

These comparisons focused less on the political strategy of the

Democratic National Committee and of the executive and more on the promise of legalization in terms of providing needed tax revenue for cash-strapped state governments and, if federal laws were amended, helping balance the federal budget.[6] While the comparison between prohibition repeal and marijuana legalization certainly has merit, it is tenuous and misleading.

At the crux of the false comparison is an oversimplification of the fundamental differences between alcohol and marijuana and their historical place in American life. There is significant evidence suggesting that the American experience with alcohol as a commodity, an intoxicant, and an object of government control is extensive and multi-faceted, leading one historian to go so far as to call the United States an "alcoholic republic."[7] Marijuana's history is quite a bit more obscured, as its place in American society, if it exists at all, typically has been relegated to the margins.[8]

MULTIPLE ORIGIN STORIES:
THE GANJA COMPLEX COMES TO THE UNITED STATES

When did marijuana first arrive in the United States? Well before the cascade of victories for the medical-marijuana movement in the twenty-first century, a long-running, multi-step process introduced the plant *cannabis sativa/indica* to the United States. Unlike the different types of alcohol introduced (cider, beer, wine, spirits), the marijuana plant's varieties had much more diverse applications, beyond its role as a source of nutrition or intoxication, as it made its way through the expanding global commodity markets during the nineteenth century.

An anthropological theory of two competing cultural streams of marijuana use in world history emerged in the 1970s and continues to underscore historical explanations of the plant's transition from a centuries-old, local, multi-use plant (the "ganja complex") to a global intoxicant (the "marijuana complex"). The emergence of the so-called marijuana complex occurred during a "psychoactive revolution" connected to the rise of global commercial capitalism that transformed several substances into global commodities. From alcohol, tobacco, and caffeine to opium, coca, and cannabis, these substances transformed the early modern world. In traditional ganja cultures, the plant operated as a vital social and cultural object with diverse uses—medicine, durable fiber, nutrition, and an occasional intoxicant, largely in ceremonial situations. As the plant entered the global flows of exchange related to the psychoactive revolution, its uses became more specific and tended to center on recreational intoxication by marginalized groups in the early twentieth century.[9]

But a closer look at the evidence complicates this story, demonstrating how the process of commodification produced curious results for a plant as widely applicable as marijuana. While the plant's diverse uses were fused together in ganja cultures, one might as well have been talking about different plants (and in a sense they were) across the so-called marijuana cultures. In the British Empire, for example, the plant was transformed from a strategic "cord of empire" (hemp), which was a staple crop in the United States from the colonial period, and the "exotic intoxicant" (marijuana) that made peasant users in India insane.[10] The problematic use by poor colonial subjects was further contrasted with the modern, increasingly professional use of psychoactive cannabis preparations by physicians and pharmacists through the nineteenth and early twentieth centuries as hashish temporarily became the recreational drug of choice among literary figures and adventurers.[11] By the time less refined, smokable marijuana arrived in the United States from Mexico and the Caribbean in the second decade of the twentieth century, the contrasting preparations were as different as smokable opium and morphine had been in the late nineteenth century.[12]

THE LONG ROAD TO THE MARIJUANA TAX ACT

The rather late introduction of recreational marijuana smoking and the plant's weak psychoactive effects compared with those of more popular drugs like opiates and to some extent cocaine relegated marijuana to the fringes of drug-use subcultures. In the context of rising activism against both alcohol and the so-called narcotic drugs, concerns over marijuana use were often overshadowed by, and occasionally subject to, concerns over other substances. This forces a reconsideration of the significance of the 1937 Marijuana Tax Act (MTA), which is often presented as the regulatory equivalent to the Eighteenth Amendment in our comparison, supposedly passed in response to a moral crisis brought on by dangerous and widespread use of the drug by Mexicans and African Americans during the so-called Reefer Madness era in the 1930s.[13]

The Marijuana Tax Act should instead be understood as more a culmination of a number of public-policy developments that followed the familiar pattern of piecemeal, state-level reforms that led to prohibition. But unlike the relative speed with which temperance advocacy turned toward prohibition in the twentieth century, the pace and circumstances of the MTA's evolution were very different.[14] Alcohol prohibition was by no means a monolithic movement, but the substance at the center of its many auxiliary concerns was always alcohol. In the case of marijuana, federal legislation evolved from more tangential regulatory concerns, such as the modernization of the medical and pharmaceutical professions, the Progressive Era push toward industry regulations, especially of food and drugs, and as a reflection of larger priorities on the national and international level with regard to controlling the opium and cocaine traffic.[15]

Thus the evolution of anti-marijuana laws was more than just a reaction to the misuse of marijuana; it was also a reaction to the misuse of opium and cocaine, on one hand, and to increased regulations on all sorts of medicinal preparations, on the other.[16] This is not to understate the importance of the racial element of this story. But unlike in the case of alcohol, in which stereotyping poor immigrant drinkers in the context of World War I perhaps tipped the scales in favor of prohibition in 1917, there was no need to tip the scales against nonmedical marijuana in 1937. It seems more likely that the use of racial stereotypes was an effort to briefly raise the profile of marijuana enough above those of the other dangerous drugs to single it out as a substance worthy of regulation.[17]

Concern over improper use of marijuana emerged from its use in medicine by some of the same individuals experimenting with hashish eating in the nineteenth century, countering the popular view that marijuana had always been an effective and widely used medicinal ingredient. The evidence suggests a more limited utility based on responses by medical professionals who used the drug and commented on its more unsettling effects. These worries culminated in a slew of poison-labeling regulations that hampered the widespread adoption of cannabis-based drugs in a rapidly professionalizing medical field.[18] By the time media attention began to focus on the nonmedical use of marijuana by Mexican migrants in the United States in the second decade of the twentieth century, the drug had all but disappeared from acceptable medical practice. By the 1930s, marijuana users were almost exclusively marijuana smokers.

In addition to the drug's increasing marginalization as a pharmaceutical drug of choice, questions regarding the regulation and control of marijuana arose in the context of the emerging international efforts to control the traffic in "dangerous" drugs. Beginning in Shanghai in 1909, the United States claimed a leadership role in the series of international discussions on drug control. Marijuana was rarely a major subject of discussion in these negotiations, but the international situation influenced domestic drug-control measures, notably the push by the Federal Bureau of Narcotics for the adoption of the Uniform State Narcotic Drug Act, which included marijuana. By 1936 the FBN chief, Harry Anslinger, had succeeded in elevating marijuana to the level of dangerous, habit-forming drug through the so-called Reefer Madness propaganda campaign. During the International Conference for the Suppression of the Illicit Traffic in Dangerous Drugs, he pushed for concrete control measures to regulate the international flows of marijuana, and for the first time nations signed agreements committing them to the suppression of marijuana use for nonmedical purposes. The MTA passed the following year.[19]

Alcohol prohibition had strong pockets of resistance, particularly in crowded urban areas, and proceeded haltingly following ratification of the constitutional amendment and subsequent enforcement regulations of prohibition. The dramatic shift in alcohol's availability required a dramatic adjustment from alcohol users in wet jurisdictions.[20] By contrast, the codification of marijuana prohibition in federal law had relatively little cultural impact. In fact, the arguments in favor of marijuana's prohibition changed dramatically after 1937.

FROM STEPPING STONE TO DECRIMINALIZATION

Following a brief crescendo of anti-marijuana discourse in the year or so following the Marijuana Tax Act, Harry Anslinger's claims that marijuana caused violence and other criminal behavior (a mark of Reefer Madness) were quickly rejected and replaced by the emphasis on an older justification for marijuana's prohibited legal status, its connection to heroin addiction. Again, marijuana control became subsumed under larger concerns about drug addiction generally. The so-called stepping-stone theory posited that prolonged exposure to marijuana led to the exposure and potential abuse of stronger drugs like heroin. Many have questioned, and continue to dispute, the stepping-stone theory, but the notion that marijuana leads to more troublesome drug use has become the standard argument against legalizing the drug and, beginning in the second half of the twentieth century, for significantly increasing the penalties for using the drug.[21]

After World War II, a spate of new drug-control laws brought more marijuana users to police attention, set new standards for the drug's illegality, and laid out stricter punishments, including mandatory minimums. Until the sixties, however, while the general use of the drug likely did increase, marijuana use remained largely relegated to isolated urban and rural subcultures.[22] A number of organized criminal organizations, drawing on resources and experience with alcohol prohibition, were able to use their wealth and infrastructure to establish distribution networks to expand the illicit market for heroin and cocaine, and marijuana entered several of these flows.[23] In these ways, early marijuana prohibition resembles alcohol prohibition. The notable exception continued to be both the low levels of overall use and the secondary role marijuana had in informing drug-control strategy.

But after a long period of marijuana being subsumed under these other concerns, popular attitudes toward the drug and its use changed in the late sixties as the United States moved rapidly from prohibition toward decriminalization of its use.[24] For the first time, the movement gained a critical mass of grass-roots support and was able to temporarily shift state resources away from enforcement of marijuana laws, even after passage of the restrictive Controlled Substances Act in 1970. The National Organization for the Reform of Marijuana Laws, created that year, and *High Times* magazine, first published in the summer of 1974, are tangible political and cultural institutions that have had long-term impacts on the debate over marijuana control.[25]

The sixties might be described as the "speakeasy era" of marijuana prohibition, as use became popular among the middle class and the harsh penalties that had targeted urban users and dealers in the previous decades drew criticism when applied to middle-class white kids. However, despite the seemingly explosive rise of middle-class marijuana users in the sixties, "respectable" use of the drug remained difficult to embrace. In the case of alcohol, the boundaries of acceptable drinking were established during the temperance movement prior to prohibition, and respectable drinkers became an important cultural and political contingency that initially subverted the consistent enforcement of prohibition and eventually provided the models for the regulatory regimes that would follow repeal. Lacking a critical mass of acceptable users prior to marijuana prohibition, new users of the drug in the sixties found it difficult to avoid those associations with subversion, and indeed the counterculture, even as they more or less successfully avoided some of the worst elements of the urban enforcement regime.

Briefly during the late sixties and the early seventies, the United States explicitly drifted toward relaxing the war on drugs, specifically the war on marijuana. John Kaplan, a California law professor and early advocate for the reform of marijuana laws, was first exposed to drug laws when in 1966 he was invited to help revise the California criminal code. Shocked by the harshness of California drug laws and informed by his experience, he published an influential book in 1970 that classified marijuana as the "New Prohibition." Kaplan sought to debunk the prevailing myths about cannabis use (it's relation to crime as well as the stepping-stone theory) and included a comprehensive discussion about the possibilities of reforming marijuana laws.

With the notable omission of state government monopolies for the distribution and sale of legal marijuana, Kaplan's reformist vision reflected much of the debate about marijuana legalization in the present. But even while going further than most of his academic colleagues (who typically stopped at decriminalization) and advocating for full legalization, he still would not acknowledge the possibility for moderate recreational use of marijuana, even though he took the same category of alcohol user as a given. Also taken for granted were the "positive values" that motivated moderate alcohol use "in terms of relaxation and lessening of anxiety." He did acknowledge that marijuana users could use the drug moderately, but it was clear that he considered even moderate use frivolous at best.[26]

The lack of models for respectable use notwithstanding, many were convinced, as many are today, that given the move toward decriminalization (seven states passed decriminalization laws in the 1970s), the "New Prohibition" was rapidly moving toward new repeal. For some, the seeming cultural and political trends toward the relaxation and possible elimination of marijuana prohibition laws supported this conclusion. Erich Goode, author of *The Marijuana Smokers,* published in 1970, echoed a common refrain in his introduction: "Marijuana use today is not a fad, not a craze. It is not going to be wished away, and legal measures to eradicate it will be only partially successful. Whether we like it or not, potsmoking [*sic*] is here to stay."[27]

It wasn't.

FROM JUST SAY NO TO JUST SAY YES: THE END OF DECRIMINALIZATION AND THE BEGINNING OF LEGALIZATION

It is important to note that the decriminalization laws passed in the 1970s were more or less in line with the new drug-control regime established by the Controlled Substances Act in 1970, specifically marijuana's Schedule I classification, which meant that it had "no currently accepted medical use and a high potential for abuse." Decriminalization maintained the "prohibition" stance by increasing enforcement against "dealers" and significantly reduced the penalties for simple possession of small amounts, presumably by "users." To some degree, this dynamic was similar to the enforcement of alcohol in some parts of the United States during prohibition. The enforcement of marijuana prohibition after 1970 focused on cross-border smuggling, as well as major grow operations in rural areas and, during the eighties and nineties, urban areas.[28] Organized parent groups and support by Nancy and Ronald Reagan kept the pressure on law enforcement to encourage children to "Just Say No!" as the strict enforcement of marijuana laws touted by drug warriors continued to skew arrest and imprisonment numbers toward poor people of color.[29]

The swing back toward decriminalization at the turn of the twenty-first century in many ways built on the temporary victories in the 1970s and gained a sense of urgency because of overenforcement against vulnerable populations. Thus, while the first decriminalization wave constituted a tacit acceptance of the drug war, this new wave is part of a growing challenge to its underlying premises. Led by HIV/AIDS and cancer patients and their caregivers and supported by social-justice movements that target the racial disparities in rates of incarceration for minor possession among their goals, grass-roots groups again lead the charge. The early medical-marijuana laws and more recent prison-reform movements, and indeed legalization, are outgrowths of these grass-roots movements, but many obstacles remain.[30]

TOWARD FULL LEGALIZATION

The rapid demise of the Eighteenth Amendment in the thirties, the complexities of the prohibition movement notwithstanding, is a testament to the central role of alcohol consumption as a generally legal, acceptable, and respectable activity for a large portion of the population. Despite its surprising and dramatic rise in the second decade of the twentieth century and the scholarly evidence of its's relative success, prohibition is remembered as a failed experiment. One hundred sixty years following passage of the first marijuana regulations, we are still trying to understand the role of marijuana in society. In the ten states that now allow recreational use and the handful of states considering full legalization, the clear articulation of that role remains elusive.

As with alcohol, the chief challenge of legalizing marijuana is the creation of a regulatory regime, as stakeholders' ideas of an ideal solution differ. The main opposition forms against the capitalist models that threaten the emergence of Big Pot, comparing those to the efforts of historically powerful drug lobbies like Big Tobacco and alcohol interests who have translated profits into political influence, in turn maintaining and expanding the various barriers to entry into the industry and decreasing regulations (many of them meant to curb harm) on existing production and sale.[31] These conflicts have played out in state-level legalization campaigns in recent years.[32] Civil rights groups oppose the continued targeting of poor urban residents for trafficking in the still extant underground market and demand that the economic benefits of legalization regimes consider and even prioritize communities affected by the failed war on drugs. Environmental groups have raised concerns about the impact of widespread legal cultivation, which can overwhelm ecosystems in outdoor grow operations and create a tremendous carbon footprint in indoor operations.[33]

There are indeed many parallels between national prohibition and the "New Prohibition." As we seem to be running headlong into new repeal, the similarities will continue to captivate observers armed with the oft-repeated adage in our field that "history repeats itself." Highlighting and emphasizing the extant superficial similarities, we ignore the complexities of both sets of debates and oversimplify the process of comprehensive regulation of substances that were, and are, relatively easy to access as long as demand exists. The difference was the source of that demand. Alcohol was ubiquitous in American life; marijuana's status was virtually the opposite of ubiquitous. Several models of respectable use of moderate amounts of alcohol for recreational, ceremonial, and even therapeutic/medicinal purposes predated prohibition and continue to define the boundaries of appropriate use. The very limited models for respectable marijuana use have only begun to emerge in the last thirty years.

The vastly different patterns of use for alcohol and marijuana influenced the rapidity and effectiveness of policy decisions. Thus, while prohibition came and went in a comparative flash, the restrictions on the cultivation, sale, and use of marijuana have held on. John Buntin, writing in *Governing Magazine,* declared in 2014 that "the notion of marijuana legalization isn't a question of if, but when."[34] But recall that Erich Goode made a very similar declaration back in 1970, just prior to Nixon's War on Drugs. Two years after Buntin's article, Donald Trump became president. He has vowed (with characteristic vacillations) to crack down on pot once again. Perhaps the better question is not when but how. And while the failures of alcohol prohibition and the conflicts that continued after repeal can provide valuable lessons about how we should legalize marijuana, we must also account for the important distinctions between the two substances that render these comparisons tenuous and misleading.

NOTES

1. Christopher S. Wren, "Votes on Marijuana Are Stirring Debate," *New York Times,* 17 November 1996.

2. Jeremy Berke, "The legal marijuana market is exploding—it'll hit almost $10 billion sales in this year," *Business Insider,* 8 December 2017.

3. "Repeal Prohibition, Again," editorial, *New York Times,* 27 July 2014.

4. Aaron F. Smith, "Legalized pot is more than a tax bonanza," *Sacramento Bee,* 5 August 2009 ("eerie"); Neal Peirce, "Should we repeal drug prohibition?," *Lawton (OK) Constitution,* 14 December 2008 ("intriguing"); "Prohibition's repeal finds a modern-day cousin,"

Lewiston (ID) Morning Tribune, 13 October 2011 ("uncanny"); Chris Woodka, "Prohibition a well-traveled road," *Pueblo (CO) Chieftain,* 17 May 2015 ("identical").

5. Smith, "Legalized pot is more than a tax bonanza"; Richard M. Evans, "A Day to Remember: Prohibition isn't Forever," *Waltham (MA) News Tribune,* 5 December 2009; Richard Evans and Steven Epstein, "What's Next for Marijuana Reform," *Fall River (MA) Herald News,* 9 January 2010; George W Liebmann, "Beyond Drug Law Reform: We Need a New Wickersham Commission," *Baltimore Sun,* 11 January 2010; "Let's be smart about how we regulate marijuana," *Honolulu Star-Advertiser,* 8 March 2011; "Prohibition's repeal finds a modern-day cousin"; John Lewallen, "Another Voice—End federal marijuana ban," *Ukiah (CA) Daily Journal,* 23 January 2012; "75 years of marijuana prohibition and we're still not protecting our children," *Portland (OR) Examiner,* 30 September 2012; Launce Rake, "All huff, no puff: Nevada's marijuana laws are a mess, to say nothing of federal laws. Will Silver State users ever get clarity?," *Bartlesville (OK) Examiner-Enterprise,* 3 April 2013; Stephen Mihm, "Marijuana's Sobering Lessons from Prohibition," *Japan Times,* 29 January 2014; "Repeal Prohibition, Again"; Woodka, "Prohibition a well-traveled road"; Rick Holmes, "Remembering Prohibition, and learning from it," *Yarmouth (MA) Register,* 27 August 2015; David L. Nathan, "Guest Commentary—As with alcohol, marijuana ban doomed to fail," *Westerly (RI) Sun,* 25 June 2016.

6. Peirce, "Should we repeal drug prohibition?"; Scott Sabatini, "Picture of Marijuana Rests in Prohibition Era," *San Francisco Examiner,* 7 March 2009; Smith, "Legalized pot is more than a tax bonanza"; Evans, "Day to Remember"; Evans and Epstein, "What's Next for Marijuana Reform"; Donald Scarinci, "Legalizing Marijuana Shows 21st Century Statesmanship," *New York Observer,* 25 May 2017.

7. William J Rorabaugh, *The Alcoholic Republic: An American Tradition* (New York: Oxford University Press, 1979). For a small sample of major historical works on alcohol, see Perry R. Duis, *The Saloon: Public Drinking in Chicago and Boston, 1880–1920* (Urbana: University of Illinois Press, 1983); David Conroy, *In Public Houses: Drink and the Revolution of Authority in Colonial Massachusetts* (Chapel Hill: University of North Carolina Press, 1995); Madelon Powers, *Faces along the Bar: Lore and Order in the Workingman's Saloon, 1870–1920* (Chicago: University of Chicago Press, 1998); Burton Peretti, *Nightclub City: Politics and Amusement in Manhattan* (Philadelphia: University of Pennsylvania Press, 2007); Michael Lerner, *Dry Manhattan: Prohibition in New York City* (Cambridge, MA: Harvard University Press, 2007); Daniel Okrent, *Last Call: The Rise and Fall of Prohibition* (New York: Scribner, 2010); Bruce E. Stewart, *Moonshiners and Prohibitionists: The Battle over Alcohol in Southern Appalachia* (Lexington: University Press of Kentucky, 2011); Richard Zacks, *Island of Vice: Theodore Roosevelt's Doomed Quest to Clean Up Sin-Loving New York* (New York: Doubleday, 2012); and Lisa McGirr, *The War on Alcohol: Prohibition and the Rise of the American State* (New York: Norton, 2016).

8. There is a growing field of historical literature on cannabis, much of which is interdisciplinary and very little of which is from historians. See Richard J. Bonnie and

Charles H. Whitebread II, *The Marijuana Conviction: A History of Marijuana Prohibition in the United States* (1974; reprint, New York: Lindesmith Center, 1999); Ernest L. Abel, *Marihuana: The First Twelve Thousand Years* (New York: Plenum, 1980); Jerome L. Himmelstein, *The Strange Career of Marihuana* (Westport, CT: Greenwood, 1983); Ralph Weisheit, *Domestic Marijuana: A Neglected Industry* (Westport, CT: Greenwood, 1992); Lester Grinspoon and James B. Bakalar, *Marihuana, the Forbidden Medicine* (New Haven, CT: Yale University Press, 1993); Isaac Campos, *Home Grown: Marijuana and the Origins of Mexico's War on Drugs* (Chapel Hill: University of North Carolina Press, 2012); Martin Booth, *Cannabis: A History* (New York: Picador, 2003); Chris S. Duvall, *Cannabis* (London: Reaktion Books, 2015); John Hudak, *Marijuana: A Short History* (Washington, DC: Brookings Institution Press, 2016); Emily Dufton, *Grass Roots: The Rise and Fall and Rise of Marijuana in America* (New York: Basic Books, 2017); and Nick Johnson, *Grass Roots: A History of Cannabis in the American West* (Corvallis: Oregon State University Press, 2017). Recent dissertations in history demonstrate the growth in the field. See Bradley J. Borougerdi, "Cord of Empire, Exotic Intoxicant: Hemp and Culture in the Atlantic World, 1600–1900" (PhD diss., University of Texas at Arlington, 2014); and Sara Elizabeth Keene, "Cultivating Illegibility: Governing the Margins of Rural Marijuana Production" (PhD diss., Cornell University, 2017). Most of the historians who write about marijuana do so in books on American drug policy at home and abroad. See David Musto, *The American Disease: Origins of Narcotic Control,* 3rd ed. (New York: Oxford University Press, 1999); William B. McAllister, *Drug Diplomacy in the Twentieth Century: An International History* (London: Routledge, 2000); David Courtwright, *Forces of Habit: Drugs and the Making of the Modern World* (Cambridge, MA: Harvard University Press, 2001); James A. Inciardi, *The War on Drugs IV: The Continuing Saga of the Mysteries and Miseries of Intoxication, Addiction, Crime, and Public Policy,* 4th ed. (Boston: Pearson, 2008); Kathleen Frydl, *The Drug Wars in America, 1940–1973* (Cambridge: Cambridge University Press, 2013); and Suzanna Reiss, *We Sell Drugs: The Alchemy of US Empire* (Oakland: University of California Press, 2014). For a botanist's perspective, see Michael Pollan, *The Botany of Desire: A Plant's-Eye View of the World* (New York: Random House, 2001).

9. Vera Rubin, ed., *Cannabis Culture* (The Hague: Mouton, 1975), 3–4. A much more recent analysis of the Ganja Complex can be found in Courtwright, *Forces of Habit,* 39–46; and Ansley Hamid, *The Ganja Complex: Rastafari and Marijuana* (Lanham, MD: Lexington Books, 2002). For examples of the global history of cannabis, see Bonnie and Whitebread, *Marijuana Conviction,* 1–5; Abel, *Marihuana;* Weisheit, *Domestic Marijuana,* 11–19; and Booth, *Cannabis,* 19–46.

10. Weisheit, *Domestic Marijuana;* Borougerdi, "Cord of Empire, Exotic Intoxicant"; Rathge, "Pondering Pot."

11. Bayard Taylor, *A Journey to Central Africa* (New York: G. P. Putnam, 1854); Taylor, *The Land of the Saracens* (New York: G. P. Putnam & Sons, 1855); Fitz H. Ludlow, *The Hasheesh Eater: Being Passages from the Life of a Pythagorean* (New York: Harper & Bros.,

1857); Victor Robinson, *An Essay on Hasheesh* (New York: Dingwall-Rock, 1925); Robert Kingman, "The Green Goddess: A Study in Dreams, Drugs and Dementia," *Medical Journal and Record* 126 (1927): 471.

12. See: Rathge, "Pondering Pot," 131–92. See also Borougerdi, "Cord of Empire, Exotic Intoxicant"; Courtwright, *Forces of Habit*, 43–46; and Bonnie and Whitebread, *Marijuana Conviction*, 48–51.

13. Musto, *American Disease*, 219–24; Himmelstein, *Strange Career of Marihuana*, 49–75; Bonnie and Whitebread, *Marijuana Conviction*, 92–153; Campos, *Home Grown*, 203–23.

14. Even more recent works overemphasize these areas. See John Kaplan, *Marijuana: The New Prohibition* (New York: World, 1970),. 89–98; Larry Sloman, *Reefer Madness: Marijuana in America* (New York: Grove, 1979), 29–83; Patrick Anderson, *High in America: The True Story Behind NORML and the Politics of Marijuana* (New York: Viking, 1981); Inciardi, *War on Drugs IV*, 30–35; and Cyril Wecht, "The Mythology of Marijuana—Let's get past the Propaganda and allow doctors to prescribe marijuana, argues forensic pathologist Cyril Wecht," *Pittsburgh Post-Gazette*, 2 March 2014.

15. Musto, *American Disease*, 221–29; McAllister, *Drug Diplomacy*, 130–31; Frydl, *Drug Wars in America*, 35–37, 52–54; Booth, *Cannabis*, 35–53; Bonnie and Whitebread, *Marijuana Conviction*, 45–91; Courtwright, *Forces of Habit*, 166–86.

16. James Harvey Young. *Toadstool Millionaires: A Social History of Patent Medicines in America before Federal Regulation* (Princeton, NJ: Princeton University Press, 1962); Joseph M. Gabriel, *Medical Monopoly: Intellectual Property Rights and the Origins of the Modern Pharmaceutical Industry* (Chicago: University of Chicago Press, 2014).

17. Bonnie and Whitebread, *Marijuana Conviction*, 175, 177–79.

18. Rathge, "Pondering Pot," 79–130. See also Booth, *Cannabis*, 120–34.

19. Bonnie and Whitebread, *Marijuana Conviction*, 79–91, 94–117.

20. For the cultural adjustment in urban places like New York, see Lerner, *Dry Manhattan*, 40–60.

21. Courtwright, *Forces of Habit*, 44, 51, 202; Bonnie and Whitebread, *Marijuana Conviction*, 204–21; Himmelstein, *Strange Career of Marihuana*, 84–89.

22. Very little scholarly attention was paid to the users themselves, particularly before 1960. Much of the existing description of this culture comes from limited source material. See Howard Becker, "Becoming a Marihuana User," *American Journal of Sociology* 59 (1953): 395–403; Himmelstein, *Strange Career of Marihuana*, 37–48; Booth, *Cannabis*; Borougerdi, "Cord of Empire, Exotic Intoxicant"; and Rathge, "Pondering Pot." Two edited collections present evidence of an extant pre-1960s user culture; the collections focus on opiate and cocaine use but also mention marijuana sparingly. See H. Wayne Morgan, ed., *Yesterday's Addicts: American Society and Drug Abuse, 1865–1920* (Norman: University of Oklahoma Press, 1974); and David Courtwright, Herman Joseph, and Don Des Jarlais, eds., *Addicts Who Survived: An Oral History of Narcotic Use in America, 1923–1965* (Knoxville: University of Tennessee Press, 1989). For rural users, see Johnson, *Grass Roots*.

23. Even less scholarly attention has been paid to the illicit market, beyond noting that it was the subject of control. See Booth, *Cannabis;* Weisheit, *Domestic Marijuana;* and Courtwright, Joseph, and Des Jarlais, *Addicts Who Survived.*

24. See Kaplan, *Marijuana;* David Solomon, *The Marijuana Papers* (Indianapolis: Bobbs-Merrill, 1966); Erich Goode, ed., *Marijuana* (New York: Atherton, 1969); Lester Grinspoon, *Marihuana Reconsidered* (Cambridge, MA: Harvard University Press, 1971); Goode, *The Marijuana Smokers* (New York: Basic Books, 1971); and Bruce D. Johnson, *Marihuana Users and Drug Subcultures* (New York: John Wiley & Sons, 1973). For the collected papers from the 1973 conference "Cross-Cultural Perspectives on Cannabis," see: Rubin, *Cannabis Culture.* See also Bonnie and Whitebread, *Marijuana Conviction,* 222–47.

25. See: Dufton, *Grass Roots.*

26. See Kaplan, *Marijuana,* ix, 311–52, quotation on 264.

27. Goode, *Marijuana Smokers,* 4; Solomon, *Marijuana Papers,* xx. For a similar sentiment today expressed by Dr. David Nathan, president of Doctors for Cannabis Regulation, see his 2016 op-ed "Cannabis has become a part of society, whether we like it or not," *Westerly (RI) Sun,* 25 June 2016. See also Maureen Turner, "Legalizing Pot: The Cork is Popping," *Valley Advocate* (Northampton, MA), 11 December 2012.

28. On decriminalization, see Musto, *American Disease,* 256–63; Bonnie and Whitebread, *Marijuana Conviction,* 222–48; Himmelstein, *Strange Career of Marihuana,* 103–6; and Frydl, *Drug Wars in America,* 347–58. On the post-1970s war on pot, see Musto, *American Disease,* 264–93; and Dufton, *Grass Roots,* 107–89.

29. Dufton, *Grass Roots,* 123–88.

30. Dufton, *Grass Roots,* 207–48; J. D. Tuccille, "Police group celebrates anniversary of Prohibition repeal with call to legalize drugs." *News & Politics Examiner,* 4 December 2008.

31. Ethan Nadelmann, "An End to Marijuana Prohibition," *National Review,* 12 July 2008; John Buntin, "Buyers & Sellers," *Governing Magazine,* 1 November 2014; Debbie Haskins, "Legalized recreational marijuana not 'inevitable,'" *Colchester (VT) Sun,* 12 November 2015; "Chronicle Recommends YES on Proposition 64," op-ed, *San Francisco Chronicle,* 15 September 2016. See also Turner, "Legalizing Pot." In early November 2015 the federal policy director of the Marijuana Policy Project, Dan Riffle, stepped down, citing conflicts with industry in setting the legalization movement in motion. See Joel Warner, "Marijuana Legalization 2015: Major Pot Activist Quits Marijuana Policy Project, Says Industry is taking over Movement," *International Business Times,* 1 December 2015.

32. Steve Elliot-Alapoet, "California Medical Association Calls for Marijuana Legalization," accessed 7 August 2018, https://www.tokeofthetown.com/2011/10/california_medical_association_calls_for_marijuana.php/; Jack Wilson, "Pot bans have precedent—Local option helps ease end of prohibition," editorial, *Eugene (OR) Register-Guard,* 14 August 2015; Gerry Tuoti and Brad Cole, "Ballot questions—Local officials weary of marijuana proposals," *Norwood (MA) Transcript & Bulletin,* 1 October 2015; "Chronicle Recommends YES on Proposition 64." Washington, DC, is a notable exception, with its unique legaliza-

tion regime. See: Mark A. R. Kleiman, "The Other Way to Legalize Marijuana—D.C. is about to make pot legal. Good, but it should keep the cannabis Industry Out." *Slate,* 4 November 2014.

33. See Johnson, *Grass Roots.*

34. Buntin, "Buyers & Sellers."

CONTRIBUTORS

Lisa M. F. Andersen is associate professor of liberal arts and history at the Julliard School in New York City. Her first book, *The Politics of Prohibition: American Governance and the Prohibition Party, 1869–1933* (Cambridge University Press, 2013), introduced the women, former abolitionists, and temperance advocates who created America's longest-lasting third party. Still interested in how Americans negotiate private issues with public stakes, she explores the history and philosophy of sex education in her forthcoming coauthored book.

Bob L. Beach received his MA from Rutgers University and is currently finishing his PhD in history at the University at Albany, SUNY. His dissertation examines the dynamics of knowledge production and consumption in regard to cannabis in New York City from 1930 to 1960. Among his recent publications are "'The big wreath, the old garland of victory': Baseball and Syracuse in 1934" (2006), The Utica College History Project; and *Happy Days Are Here Again: Utica and Prohibition,* a radio documentary broadcast on WAMC, Northeast Public Radio, 2006.

Joe L. Coker is the author of *Liquor in the Land of the Lost Cause: Southern White Evangelicals and the Prohibition Movement* (University Press of Kentucky, 2007). Raised in Tennessee, he received his PhD from Princeton Theological Seminary and is now a senior lecturer in the Department of Religion at Baylor University. His work focuses on how religion and the surrounding culture shape and impact each other. He has published an exhaustive bibliography of the temperance hymnals mentioned in his essay and is currently working on a chapter on Christian fundamentalists and alcohol for the forthcoming *Oxford Handbook of Christian Fundamentalism.*

Richard F. Hamm is professor of history at the University at Albany, SUNY. Raised in the Bronx and in Florida, he received his PhD in American history from the University of Virginia under the direction of Charles W. McCurdy. He is the author of *Shaping the Eighteenth Amendment: Temperance Reform, Legal Culture, and the Polity, 1880–1920* (University of North Carolina Press, 1995); "*Olmstead v. United States:* The Constitutional Challenges of Prohibition Enforcement," a unit of the "Teaching the History of the Federal Courts" project of the Federal Judicial Center; and "Short Euphorias Followed by Long Hangovers: Unintended Consequences of the Eighteenth and Twenty-first Amendments," in *Unintended Consequences of Constitutional Amendments,* ed. David E. Kyvig (University of Georgia Press, 2000), along with articles on prohibition, legal history, and civil liberties.

Michael Lewis is professor of sociology at Christopher Newport University in Virginia. Raised in Yonkers, New York, and Denver, Colorado, he earned his BA in history at the University of Colorado and both his MA and PhD in sociology from the University of Virginia. He is the author of *The Coming of Southern Prohibition: The Dispensary System and the Battle over Liquor in South Carolina, 1907–1915* (Louisiana State University Press, 2016). His current work examines the changes in drinking habits in South Carolina during the dispensary period.

Garrett Peck is an author, historian, and tour guide in the Washington, DC, area. He has published seven books, including *The Prohibition Hangover: Alcohol in America from Demon Rum to Cult Cabernet* (2009), *Prohibition in Washington D.C.: How Dry We Weren't* (2011), *Capital Beer: A Heady History of Brewing in Washington, D.C.* (2014), and most recently,

The Great War in America: World War I and Its Aftermath (2018). His temperance tour of prohibition sites in the nation's capital has been featured on C-SPAN Book TV and on the History Channel series *Ten Things You Don't Know About*. Peck is a veteran of the US Army. He received his BA from the Virginia Military Institute and his MA from George Washington University. He has lectured at the Library of Congress, at the National Archives, and for the Smithsonian Associates and often speaks to historical societies, literary clubs, and trade associations.

Thomas R. Pegram is professor of history at Loyola University Maryland. Raised in the Midwest and in California, he received his PhD in the history of American civilization at Brandeis University under the direction of Morton Keller. He is the author of *Partisans and Progressives: Private Interest and Public Policy in Illinois, 1870–1922* (University of Illinois Press, 1992), *Battling Demon Rum: The Struggle for a Dry America, 1800–1933* (Ivan R. Dee, 1998), and *One Hundred Percent American: The Rebirth and Decline of the Ku Klux Klan in the 1920s* (Ivan R. Dee, 2011), along with articles and essays on prohibition, 1920s social movements, and American politics and governance in the late nineteenth and early twentieth centuries.

Mark Lawrence Schrad is associate professor of political science at Villanova University. He received his PhD from the University of Wisconsin. His books include *The Political Power of Bad Ideas: Networks, Institutions, and the Global Prohibition Wave* (2010) and *Vodka Politics: Alcohol, Autocracy, and the Secret History of the Russian State* (2014), both published by Oxford University Press. His current project is a global history of temperance and prohibition politics, to be published by Oxford University Press in 2019.

Ann-Marie E. Szymanski is associate professor of political science at the University of Oklahoma. She holds a PhD in government from Cornell University. She is the author of *Pathways to Prohibition: Radicals, Moderates, and Social Movement Outcomes* (Duke University Press,

2003), as well as several articles and papers that explore the interplay between associations, state structure, and policymaking. She is currently working on a book manuscript that examines the role of private groups in the creation and enforcement of American regulatory policies.

H. Paul Thompson Jr. is dean of humanities and professor of history at North Greenville University. His research focuses on nineteenth-century temperance, especially the intersection of temperance, religion, and race relations in the New South. Among his publications are *"A Most Stirring and Significant Episode": Religion and the Rise and Fall of Prohibition in Black Atlanta, 1865–1887* (Northern Illinois University Press, 2013) and "Temperance and Prohibition," in the *Oxford Research Encyclopedia of American History*. He earned his PhD in American history at Emory University.

INDEX

AAPA. *See* Association Against the Prohibition Amendment (AAPA)

abolitionism, 9, 24, 26–27

abstinence: from distilled spirits, 3, 25; Gandhi and, 123–24; ideology and, 33; individual, 54; prohibition and, 72, 111; temperance and, 4–5, 7, 10–11, 16, 135

abstinence pledge, 3, 7, 10, 16, 141. *See also* sobriety pledge; teetotal pledge

Addams, Jane, 31

addiction, 72, 135, 140, 144, 146, 152

African Americans, 12, 95, 150. *See also* race

African Methodist Episcopal churches, 6

Age of Reason, 23–24

Albert, King of Belgium, 117

alcohol beverage control (ABC) regulatory regimes, 134. *See also* regulation of alcohol

alcohol consumption: campaigns against individual drinking, 37–38, 41–42, 49–50 (*see also* abstinence; Anti-Saloon League of America [ASL]; temperance movement); changes in, after repeal of prohibition, 131–42; dangers of, 22–25, 72–73, 111; at home, 135; individual, 37–38, 41–42, 49–50; locations for,

138–39 (*see also* bars; saloons; speakeasies); moderation in, 24–25; positive attributes of, 23; as respectable, 153, 156–57; sales records and, 68; as sinful, 6, 30, 42, 142; social and economic costs of, 22–25, 28, 39, 72–73

alcohol consumption rates: antebellum, 3; during prohibition era, 66–73, 89; repeal of prohibition and, 139–40

Alcoholics Anonymous (AA), 140–41

alcohol industry: capitalist greed and, 31; lobbying by, 156; marketing by, 135–36; vertical integration of, 133. *See also* brewers and breweries; distillers; liquor traffic; liquor trust; retail liquor business; saloons; wineries

alcoholism, 42, 140–41

alcohol poisoning, 111

Alee, William S., 58

American Baptist Home Mission, 6

American Bar Association, 101

American Board of Commissioners for Foreign Missions, 5, 6

American Federation of Labor, 101

American Issue, 15, 39, 48

American Legion, 101

American Missionary Association, 6

American Sunday School Union, 5–6
American Temperance Society, 4–6
American Temperance Union, 5, 6, 9. *See
   also* National Temperance Society &
   Publication House (NTS&PH)
American Tract Society, 5–6
Anderson, William H., 41, 56
Anheuser-Busch, 136
Anslinger, Harry, 151, 152
anticolonialism, 121–25
Anti-Lottery Act (1895), 64n16
Anti-Saloon League of America (ASL):
   Congressional support for, 92; found-
   ing of, 12–13; goals of, 2–3, 38–43, 49;
   lobbying by, 41, 47–48, 99, 101; loss of
   vitality, 99; political theory of, 43–48;
   progressive evangelism and, 32; prohi-
   bition enforcement and, 79; strategies,
   47–50, 55–59; temperance movement
   and, 15–17
Archibald, A. C., 106–7, 109
ASL. *See* Anti-Saloon League of America
   (ASL)
Association Against the Prohibition
   Amendment (AAPA), 90, 94–103
Atlanta, GA, 12

Baby Boomers, 137
Baltimore, MD, 94
Baptists, 6, 11, 22, 26, 42, 133
Bark, Pyotr Lvovich, 110
bars, 139. *See also* saloons
bathtub gin, 132, 134
Beck, James M., 96
Beecher, Lyman, 3–4
beer: craft and microbrewing, 136–37;
   German immigrants and, 8, 55, 134;
   Icelandic ban on, 118; lager, 134, 136;
   low-alcohol, 132–33; male drinkers of,
   136; marketed as temperance drink,

62; moderate consumption of, 25; near
   beer, 67; positive attributes of, 24. *See
   also* brewers and breweries
beer can, invention of, 135
BEER Group, 92
Belgium, 117
"Benevolent Empire," 1
Big Tobacco, 156
Bill W. (William Wilson), 140
Blocker, Jack, 46
blue laws, 141. *See also* regulation of
   alcohol
Bolshevik Revolution (1917), 112, 114–15
Boole, Ella, 135
bootlegging, 76–77, 85, 132, 134, 138
Borah, William, 94
bourbon, 137
Brandeis, Louis, 85
brawling, 25
brewers and breweries: after repeal of
   prohibition, 135–39; German American,
   55; industry organizations, 13; market-
   ing by, 135–36; opposition to prohibi-
   tion, 44, 62; saloons owned by, 89–90;
   tasting rooms, 138–39; trusts and, 45.
   See also alcohol industry; beer
Brewers Association, 137
bribery, 80
British Empire, 123–25, 149
Brooks Law (1887), 57
Brown, John, 26
Bruce, William Cabell, 92
Brussels International Conference (1889),
   108
Bryce law (1904), 57
Buntin, John, 157
Bureau of Prisons, 84
Bureau of Prohibition, 92–93
Burns, Ken, 1
Business Insider, 145

California: drug laws, 154; prohibition enforcement, 94; Proposition 215 (medical marijuana), 145, 147; wineries, 138
Canada, 22, 106–7, 119–20
Canada Temperance Act (Scott Act), 120
cannabis sativa/indica. See marijuana
Cannon, James, Jr., 99
capitalism, 31, 112, 113, 148
Capone, Al, 78
carceral state, 76, 87; development of, 83–84. *See also* incarceration
Carroll v. United States, 85
Carter, Jimmy, 136
Cartwright, Peter, 6
centralized government, 96–97. *See also* federal government
Charleston, South Carolina, Temperance Union, 6
Charrington, Ernest, 44
Chicago, IL, 58, 78
child labor ban, 96
Choate, Joseph H., Jr., 101–2
Christians: religious conservatives, 20–34; temperance and, 6, 11. *See also* Baptists; evangelical Protestants; Lutherans; Methodists; Presbyterians; Roman Catholics
Christian Socialism, 29
cider, 35n16
cirrhosis, deaths from, 68–70
civil-service laws, 79–80
Civil War, 28
Clark, J. Henry, 8
Coast Guard, 79
cocaine, 135, 149–50, 152
cocktail culture, 137–38
colonialism, 121–25, 149
Colorado, 145, 147
Communications Act (1934), 85

Congregationalists, 6
Congress, US: federal prisons and, 84; passage of prohibition amendment, 16–17; prohibition enforcement and, 80; repeal and, 102. *See also* House of Representatives, US; Senate, US
Constitutional amendments, 59–62, 84–86, 95–96. *See also* Eighteenth Amendment; Twenty-First Amendment
constitutional-law doctrines, 76, 84–86
Controlled Substances Act (1970), 153, 155
Control States, 133–34. *See also* dispensary system
corporations, 13
corruption: federal court cases on, 82; organized crime and, 78; political, 46; in prison management, 83; prohibition and, 73, 97, 99, 132, 147; vice and, 77
counterculture, 153
county option (Ohio), 56
craft-brewing industry, 136–37
crime: cider and, 35n16; hard liquor and, 25; liquor traffic and, 46; marijuana and, 152, 154; before prohibition, 77–78; war against, 87
criminal justice system, 92. *See also* enforcement; incarceration
cultural norms, 131, 140–42
Cummings, Homer, 87
Curran, Henry, 101
Customs Office, 79
Cuyler, Theodore, 12

Darrow, Clarence, 91
deaths: from bad liquor, 73; from cirrhosis, 68–70. *See also* health issues
decriminalization of marijuana, 153–55
Defender, 41
democracy: culture of, 8; grass-roots, 14; liquor traffic and, 43–46

Democratic Party: enforcement and, 92–93; liquor traffic and, 44; marijuana legalization and, 147–48; Prohibition Party and, 45; repeal and, 101–3, 132

Department of Scientific Temperance Instruction, 10

Detroit, MI, 94

Dickmeyer, William, 89

disease, 46

dispensary system, 57. *See also* Control States; Gothenburg system

distilled spirits: abstinence from, 3, 25; consumption after repeal of prohibition, 134–39; dangers of, 23–25; drinking habits and, 134–35; per capita consumption of, 25; prescribed for medicinal use, 67

distillers: opposition to prohibition, 44, 62; tasting rooms, 139; trade associations, 13, 136. *See also* alcohol industry; liquor traffic; liquor trust

distribution system, 62; regulation of, 133

Dobyns, Fletcher, 98

"Do Everything" (WCTU motto), 10, 29

Dominion Alliance for the Total Suppression of the Liquor Traffic, 120

Dow, Neal, 8, 27–28

Dr. Bob (Robert Smith), 140

drinking. *See* alcohol consumption; drunkenness

drinking age, 142

drug abuse, 146. *See also* addiction

drug lobbies, 156

drugs, illegal, 78, 81

drug wars, modern, 38, 135, 144–57

drunk driving, 142

drunkenness: arrests for, 25, 69–71, 119; attitudes toward, 140; cider and, 35n16; opposition to, 3; prohibition agents

fired for, 80; during prohibition era, 38; reformed-drunkard testimonials, 7; in Russia/Soviet Union, 110, 112–13; saloons and, 40, 42

dry communities, 12, 46, 54, 107, 141

dry households, 54

drys (supporters of prohibition): diversity in, 22–23. *See also* Anti-Saloon League of America (ASL); Prohibition Party; temperance movement; Woman's Christian Temperance Union (WCTU)

due process rights, 86–87

Duis, Perry, 40

Du Pont, Irénée, 96, 98

Du Pont, Lammot, 96

Du Pont, Pierre, 96, 97–98

economic collapse, 90, 98–99. *See also* Great Depression

Edge, Walter E., 92

education, on alcohol and drugs, 10–11, 72, 144–45

Edwards, Edward I., 92, 95

Edwards, Justin, 6

Eighteenth Amendment: enforcement of (*see* enforcement; federal police; prohibition agents; Volstead Act); legalized beer and, 132–33; passage of, 2–3, 16–17, 32; ratification by states, 49; repeal of (*see* repeal of prohibition). *See also* prohibition movement

employers, temperance and, 25–26

enforcement: by federal police, 78–81 (*see also* federal police; prohibition agents); federal prosecutors and, 81–82; by localities, 41, 78, 94–95; of marijuana prohibition, 147, 155; nullification and, 94–95; problems associated with, 89–95, 99, 147; small-scale violations and, 77; in Soviet Union, 113; by states, 79–80, 91, 94

England, 106

Enlightenment, 24

environmental issues, 17, 156

Episcopalians, 11

Estonia, 116–17

Europe, prohibition in, 107–21

evangelical Protestants: conservative fundamentalist, 20–22, 30–34; liberal modernist, 30–34; prohibition and, 20–34, 108; temperance and, 4, 11, 20–22, 25–27

excise tax, 61, 123–24. *See also* tax revenue

Extraordinary Commission for Combatting Counter-Revolution and Sabotage (CheKa), 112–13

February Revolution (1917), 112, 115. *See also* Bolshevik Revolution (1917)

Federal Bureau of Investigation (FBI), 78–80, 87

Federal Bureau of Narcotics, 151

federal government: authority of, 96–97; limits on, 59–60; social reform and, 17

federal police: expansion of, 76, 78–81, 86–87; power of, 59–60; supervised by federal jurists, 86. *See also* enforcement; prohibition agents

federal prison population, 83–84, 87, 92

federal prosecutors, 81–82

fentanyl, 135

Fifteen Gallon Law (1838), 8

Fifteenth Amendment, 95

Fifth Amendment, 85

Finland, 22, 114–16

Finney, Charles, 6, 25–26

Fisher, Irving, 91–92

food conservation, 55

Foster, J. Ellen, 11, 14

Fourteenth Amendment, 95

Fourth Amendment, 84–86

France, 106, 119

Frankfurter, Felix, 95

Friedman, Lawrence M., 78

Fugitive Slave Law, 94

gambling, 39, 62, 77–78

Gandhi, Mahatma, 123–24

gang violence, 73, 78, 87

ganja complex, 148–49

Garrison, William Lloyd, 26

Gatch, John N., 63

Gatch, Lewis and Mary, 54, 63, 63n1

German-American Alliance (GAA), 55

German immigrants, 8, 55, 62, 134

Germany, 106, 116, 117, 120

Gerrans, Orpha, 63

Gillett, Frederick, 61

gin, 137; "bathtub gin," 132, 134

Goode, Erich, 154, 157

Goremykin, Ivan, 112

Gothenburg system, 118. *See also* dispensary system

government: bans and restrictions on products, 33–34; democracy and, 8, 14, 43–46; intervention in national economy, 55; rise of bureaucracies, 13

Government of India Act (1935), 124

Grand National Assembly (GNA), 122

Granholm v. Heald, 139

Grantham, Dewey, 20–21

grass-roots democracy, 14

Great Depression, 98–99; alcohol regulations and, 134; beer consumption during, 135; global, 116; repeal of prohibition and, 90, 102–3, 132

Greatest Generation, 136, 137

Republican Party, 9; enforcement of prohibition and, 90, 92–93; liquor traffic and, 44; Prohibition Party and, 45; repeal and, 101–2, 132; women in, 100
residence-district option (Ohio), 56
retail liquor business, 7; prohibition era and, 67; regulation of, 133–34
retail liquor licenses, 43–45, 57, 62, 133
revivalists, 25–26; fire-and-brimstone, 20, 26, 30, 33; temperance and, 3–4, 6
Riffle, Dan, 161n31
rights, individual, 84–86
Robinson, Joseph, 101
Rochester, NY, 25–26
Rockefeller, John D., Jr., 133
Rockefeller, John D., Sr., 39
Roman Catholics, 8, 11
Romanov, Konstantin Konstantinovich, 109–10
Romanov, Oleg Konstantinovich, 110
Roosevelt, Franklin Delano, 102, 132–33
Rorabaugh, William J., 77, 139
rum, 137
Rush, Benjamin: *Inquiry into the Effects of Spiritous Liquors,* 3, 23–26
Russell, Howard, 13–15, 17, 32
Russell, John, 44
Russian Empire, 106, 109–16
Russo-Japanese War (1904–5), 110
Rutgers University Center of Alcohol Studies, 140

Sabbatarians, 134
Sabin, Charles H., 96, 100
Sabin, Pauline, 100
saloons: election polling places in, 44; elimination of, 89–90, 135; licensing fees, 43–44; as male-only spaces, 39–40, 139; model, 62; opposition to, 38–43,

50, 139 (*see also* Anti-Saloon League of America [ASL])
San Francisco, CA, 94
Saudi Arabia, 108
Schlitz, 136
Schouse, Jouett, 102
scientific discovery, 23–24
Scopes trial, 30
search-and-seizure doctrine, 84–86
Second Great Awakening, 3, 25, 33
Secret Service, 78
sellers. *See* retail liquor business
Senate, US, 17, 38, 48–49, 55, 93. *See also* Congress, US
senators, direct election of, 60
Seventeenth Amendment, 60
Sheppard, Morris, 47
sin, alcohol consumption as, 6, 30, 42, 142
single-issue pressure groups. *See* Anti-Saloon League of America (ASL)
Sixteenth Amendment, 60, 61–62
slavery, abolition of, 9, 24, 26–27
Smith, Al, 95, 101
Smith, Robert (Dr. Bob), 140
smuggling, 81, 115, 116, 119, 155
sobriety pledge, 42. *See also* abstinence pledge; teetotal pledge
social and economic costs: of alcohol, 22–25, 28, 34, 39, 46, 72–73; of marijuana, 146
social drinking, 142. *See also* alcohol consumption
Social Gospel, 31
socialism, 29, 31
social movements: constitutional amendments and, 60–61; goals of, 73; prohibition and, 22, 31
Sonoma County, CA, 138
Sons of Temperance, 7

South: local-option laws, 56; statewide prohibition campaigns, 56

South Africa, 123

South Carolina, 57

southerners, prohibition and, 21, 28, 95

Soviet Union, 112–14

Spain, 118, 119

speakeasies, 132, 139

Stalin, Joseph, 113

state constitutions, 60; prohibition and, 11–12; regulations in, 64n19

state conventions, 90

state governments: enforcement and, 79–80, 91, 94; and marijuana legalization, 145, 147, 156

state prison populations, 83–84

state prohibition laws, 8, 16, 27–28, 101; Anti-Saloon League and, 56–59; in early twentieth century, 30; in Maine, 8, 12, 27; and referendum campaigns, 48

state-run liquor stores, 57, 133–34

Stayton, William, 96

Stelzle, Charles, 31, 39

stepping-stone theory, 152, 154

Stone, Harlan Fiske, 81–82

Strong, Josiah, 31

suffrage, women's. *See* women's suffrage movement

Sunday, Billy, 30, 135

Sunday alcohol sales, 134, 141. *See also* regulation of alcohol

Supreme Court, US, 60, 65n22, 91–92

Sweden, 107–8, 118

Szymanski, Ann-Marie, 125

Taft, William Howard, 91

tax revenue: alcohol and, 73, 86, 98–99, 103, 132; excise tax, 61, 123–24; federal income tax, 60, 61–62, 98–99; liquor licenses, 44–45; marijuana and, 148

Taylor v. United States, 85

teetotalism, 11, 21

teetotal pledge, 5–7. *See also* abstinence pledge; sobriety pledge

temperance movement: antebellum, 3–8; diverse supporters of, 22–23; eighteenth-century origins, 23–25; end of, 135; goals and strategies of, 1–18 (*see also* abstinence); hymnals, 21; in Iceland, 118; postbellum, 9–12; progressives in, 23–25; prohibition movement and, 1–3, 7–8, 12–18, 27–30 (*see also* prohibition movement); in Russia, 109; transnational, 107, 117. *See also* Anti-Saloon League of America (ASL); Woman's Christian Temperance Union (WCTU)

temperance newspapers, 26

Tennessee, 12

Tenth Amendment, 59

tequila, 137

Texas, 12

three-tier system, 133–34, 138–39. *See also* regulation of alcohol

Tillman, Ben, 57

Tinkham, George, 95

Torrio, Johnny, 78

Towards Liquor Control (1933), 133

Trader Vic's, 137

Treasury Department, US, 92

Trotsky, Leon, 113

Trump, Donald, 146, 157

trust-busting, 13

trusts, liquor, 13–15, 45

Turkey, 121–23

Twenty-First Amendment, 90, 100, 102, 133